'THE WINGS OF THE SPRIRIT'
EXPLORING FEMININE SYMBOLISM
IN EARLY PNEUMATOLOGY

ESWTR Studies in Religion

Published *sub aegis* of the European Society of Women in Theological Research

1. Julie Hopkins, '*The Wings of the Spirit'—Exploring Feminine Symbolism in Early Pneumatology: A Reassessment of a Key Metaphor in the Spiritual Teachings of the* Marcarian Homilies *in the Light of Early Syriac Christian Tradition*, Louvain: Peeters, 2020.
2. Antonina Wozna, *Némesis: Modelo de justicia de Mary Daly*, Louvain: Peeters (forthcoming).
3. Theresa Yugar, Lilian Dube, Teresia Hinge, and Sarah Robinson-Bertoni (eds.), *Valuing Lives, Healing Earth. Festschrift in Honour of Rosemary Radford Ruether*, Vol. 1 and 2, Louvain: Peeters (forthcoming).

‘THE WINGS OF THE SPIRIT’ EXPLORING FEMININE SYMBOLISM IN EARLY PNEUMATOLOGY

A Reassessment of a Key Metaphor in the Spiritual Teachings of the *Macarian Homilies* in the Light of Early Syriac Christian Tradition

Julie M. Hopkins

PEETERS
LEUVEN – PARIS – BRISTOL, CT
2020

ISBN 978-90-429-4113-7
eISBN 978-90-429-4122-9
D/2020/0602/15

A catalogue record for this book is available from the Library of Congress.

'As the wings of the doves over their nestlings,
and the mouths of their nestlings towards their mouths,
so are the wings of the Spirit over my heart.'

Odes of Solomon 28:1

EDITOR'S PREFACE

In the early nineties, I had the pleasure to meet Dr. Julie M. Hopkins on multiple occasions. In those days, Julie was working in the Netherlands on Christology. In 1994, her work was published under the title: *Towards a Feminist Christology. Jesus of Nazareth, European Women, and the Christological Crisis* (Kampen: Kok Pharos, 1994), with William B. Eerdmans Publishing Company (Grand Rapids, MI) publishing the American version in 1995. And Julie did not stop developing her important thinking. With this book, 'The Wings of the Spirit' — Exploring Feminine Symbolism in Early Pneumatology, she contributes towards the development of a revitalised pneumatology!

It is an absolute honour and pleasure to have this book published as the first in a new series: the *ESWTR Studies in Religion*, with ESWTR standing for the European Society of Women in Theological Research.

The editorial board, Gertraud Ladner (Innsbruck), Nicola Slee (Birmingham/Amsterdam) and Kristin De Troyer (Salzburg), are looking forward to receiving many wonderful manuscripts and publishing the best monographs and edited volumes produced by women!

September 5, 2019
Kristin De Troyer
President of the European Society of Women
in Theological Research

AUTHOR'S PREFACE

This book is the culmination of my life-long interest in early Christian religious experience and women's studies. It began as a series of research projects at the University of Wales in Lampeter (now the University of Trinity St. David). Originally I was seeking to understand the religious beliefs and experiences of the Celtic hermit saints of the 4th - 6th centuries. It became clear that their 'desert spirituality' was rooted in the eremetical practices of the eastern Mediterranean. So I began to try and understand the evolution of the anchoretic monasticism of the 'desert fathers and mothers' of Egypt and was finally led further east to the Syrian Orient and the original Jewish-Christian migrants from Palestine.

Thanks to the pioneering work of translators such as Sebastian Brock and Robert Murray, the Syriac hymnody of Ephrem was at last becoming available in English, although it has always been well known in the Eastern Orthodox family of churches. I found the Syriac tradition with its rich treasury of spiritual teaching and holistic liturgical rituals a welcome source of inspirational insights and practices which have renewed my own beliefs. In particular, its emphasis upon a charismatic and fully embodied encounter with the dynamism and transformative grace of the Holy Spirit was both personally challenging and enlightening. The feminine name and functions of the Spirit helped to shift my theology from a critical feminist deconstruction of patriarchal and androcentric God-language towards a reclaiming of my Christian heritage as a spiritual resource for today. However, it still continues to raise the whole question of how to deal with the issue of gender in translation and how to integrate the feminine divine into church liturgy, hymnody and preaching.

The collections of 'Macarian Homilies' (*Macriana*) have played an important role in Greek hesychast and Slavic spirituality. Their teaching upon the centrality of the heart, the 'divine light of Tabor' and mystical communion with the indwelling Spirit are to this day, part and parcel of eastern monasticism. In the West, their influence can be traced in writers as disparate as Benedict, Dante, John Wesley and Kierkegaard and their emphasis upon a personal intimate relationship with God and spiritual plenitude has inspired Spiritual Franciscans, Jesuits and Protestant Pietism. Today, the subjective and conversational style of the homilies with their teaching on the daily gracious gifting of personal guidance and empowerment by the Spirit, seem out of kilter with the critical study of the doctrine of the Holy Spirit (pneumatology) in academic theology.

This study is my post-doctoral thesis (D.D.Lic.), but I have sought to add more commentary and some explanatory notes on the technical language in the hope that it might appeal to a wider readership. Its aim is to trace the evolution and influence of the metaphor of the 'wings of the Spirit' from the eastern Syriac tradition, via the Macarian spiritual homilies, to the Greek Cappadocian Fathers who added the clause on the Holy Spirit to the Nicene Creed. My approach has been as an engaged historian of Christian religious experience. I have attempted to describe, interpret and compare the insights on the Holy Spirit of teachers from within their own 4th century AD Syriac and Greek cultural and religious contexts. My method does not aim at scientific analysis of the phenomenology or psychology of their spiritual experiences, rather it focuses upon their usage of the 'wings of the Spirit' metaphor and explores how this evocative symbol generated a religious conversation and theological innovation, East and West. The academic, *Abstract*, which describes succinctly my aims and methodology follows, but I have also added an extended explanatory in the *Introduction*.

Many friends and colleagues have supported my research over the years. I would like to thank my tutor, Dr. Andreas Andreopoulos, and examiner, Dr. Marcus Plested. Dr. John Court helped with the translation of difficult Greek passages in the Macarian texts. My friend and patroness, Dr. Elinor Kapp supported my research financially. I thank my colleagues, Dr. Lene Sørjup and Prof. Kristin De Troyer for finally persuading me to publish. Throughout this decade I have had the great privilege of being guided by the hesychast hermit, Hieromonk Silouan, who has tried to teach me how to bring these insights from my head into my heart.

This book is dedicated to my late mother, Joyce Hopkins, in whose home and company I spent the years of my research.

Julie M. Hopkins

CONTENTS

PART III: A Macarian Synthesis of Syriac and Greek Wings Metaphors?

ABSTRACT

'The Wings of the Spirit' A Reassessment of a Key Metaphor in the *Macarian Homilies* in the Light of Early Christian Syriac Tradition

This study challenges the view of current scholarship that the frequent 'wings of the Spirit' metaphor in the homilies of the anonymous fourth century writer, 'Pseudo-Macarius', was an appropriation of the Christianised version of the Platonic 'wings of the soul', as utilised in the Alexandrian School of Origen and Gregory of Nyssa. In this thesis an alternative cultural and religious tradition is advocated as the source, namely early Syriac Christianity. I demonstrate that in that context, the metaphor of the 'wings of the Spirit' and the related symbol of the 'hovering' wings of the Spirit, were evoked in sacramental liturgies, and proto-monastic rites of initiation, praised in hymnody and utilised in teaching on prayer and spiritual states of inspiration and contemplation. In Part I, this tradition is described with examples from Ephrem the Syrian and Aphrahat the Persian Sage. In Part II, I demonstrate that it is possible to interpret the four main clusters of teachings on the 'wings of the Spirit' in the *Macarian Homilies* from within this cultural and religious tradition. Further, that in the Macarian usage, this teaching is closely linked to some other key themes in Syriac ascetic tradition, namely the nature and functions of the Spirit as a mother, or mother-bird, elements of realised eschatology linked with 'mother Jerusalem' and the 'hidden church' of the heart. In Part III, I discuss the hermeneutical and methodological issues this new perspective offers in the context of the scholarly debate concerning the relationship between the *Macriana* and the Cappadocian Fathers. In particular, I re-examine the presupposition that Macarian 'wings language' was borrowed from the writings of Gregory of Nyssa and was bedded within a spiritual and ascetic framework deriving ultimately from Cappadocian teaching. My conclusion is that the Macarian metaphor, written in Greek but deriving from a Syro-Mesopotamian context, offered a flexible pan-cultural verbal icon that creatively interpreted the Christian experience of the Holy Spirit in the Orient to Hellenic Christianity.

Julie Marina Hopkins
Trinity St. David
University of Wales in Lampeter

INTRODUCTION

The Wings of the Spirit

The *Macarian Homilies* as a Flight Path of the Holy Spirit from Eastern Heart to Western Mind?

In this study I explore the evocative metaphor of the, 'wings of the Spirit' in the spiritual teaching of the late 4th century collection of anonymous writings, the *Macarian Homilies*. This corpus of four surviving manuscripts of sermons and sayings, the so-called, ***Macriana***, were originally daily writings produced under inspiration by a Christian teacher for his disciples. Although the sayings were later attributed to the Egyptian Desert Father Macarius the Great of Skete, the teacher is now believed to have lived in the Greek-speaking Roman province of Syria, probably near the great Christian centre of Antioch.[1]

The *Macarian Homilies* were written in the Greek language but reflect a thought-world and ethos derived from the traditions of the Syro-Mesopotamian Christian Orient further east. In this vast region straddling the Sassanid Persian Empire and Roman Syria, the *lingua franca* since the 6th century B.C., was Syriac, a dialect of Semitic Aramaic. In Syriac, as in Aramaic, the language of Jesus and the first Palestinian Christians, the grammatical gender of God's Holy Spirit, 'the Spirit of Holiness' was feminine. The Christian Church of the Syrian Orient used the image of the 'hovering' wings of a mother bird to symbolise its understanding of the presence and efficacy of the Holy Spirit in and through the sacraments. The specific metaphor of the 'wings of the Spirit' was frequently cited in the devotional literature of poetry, hymnody, metrical homilies and spiritual treatises, in particular to describe spiritual states of grace, inspiration and contemplation. It was also associated with the consecrated life of Christian virgins, the so-called 'Sons and Daughters of the Covenant' (*bnai/bnat qeiãmã*) and with eschatological hopes for the resurrection of the dead in Paradise.

1. In the 4th century, Greek was the spoken and literary language in Roman Syria, west of the River Euphrates, see Sebastian Brock, "Greek and Syriac in Late Antique Syria", in A.K. Bowman & Greg Woolf (eds.), *Literacy and Power in the Ancient World* (Cambridge: Cambridge University Press, 1994), 149-60.

This remarkable development was influenced by the translation of the Hebrew Bible into written Syriac, the literary Aramaic dialect of Edessa. Edessa, "the Athens of the East" (modern day Urfa in Turkey) had been colonised by Jewish merchants and later migrants of the Diaspora for centuries. How Christians arrived in the region is a scholarly debate.[2] Their Jewish-Christian worldview suggests conversion locally from Judaism, but the founding myth of Edessene Christianity was that the Apostle Judas Thomas sent his disciple Addai to evangelise the area. Addai, through his healing and teaching converted the local king.[3] The work of translating the Masoretic Hebrew Bible into Syriac, the *Peshitta*, was begun by Jewish exegetes but at some point they abandoned the labour and it was continued by Christians who also added New Testament writings.[4] The *Peshitta,* reflected lines of interpretation deriving from *Targumim*, rabbinic Aramaic paraphrases of Hebrew texts. These Semitic oral traditions stretched back to the earlier Palestinian milieu of both primitive Christianity and Jewish sectarianism, including Qumran.

In the *Peshitta*, the grammatically feminine name for the 'Holy Spirit' (*rûhâ qaddishta*), leant authority to the Syriac Christian usage of the metaphorical terminology of the wings and played an important part in its evolution.[5] Susan Ashbrook Harvey notes that while the portrayal of the Spirit using feminine images arose from 'the simple grammatical clue that the Spirit, its adjectives and verbs, were all in the feminine gender', since Semitic verbs are inflected by gender, a religious vocabulary in Syriac developed. Hence verbs describing the Spirit's actions, such as 'to come upon', 'dwell in', 'search', 'lead', and the dominant sacramental image, 'to hover' (*rahep*), were conjugated in the feminine.[6]

The *Macarian Homilies*, were written in Greek, and therefore generally use the neuter gender for the Holy Spirit (ἅγιον πνεῦμα). However, there is a clear tendency to use maternal language to describe the functions and

2. Robert Murray, *Symbols of Church and Kingdom: A Study in Early Syriac Tradition* (London, T & T Clark, 2006), 4-9.

3. *The Teaching of Addai*, English trans. George Howard, SBL Texts and Translations 16; Early Christian Literature series 4 (Michigan, Scholars Press, 1981).

4. This thesis has been advocated by Michael Weitzman in a number of articles since 1992 and in his major work, *The Syriac Version of the Old Testament: An Introduction* (Cambridge, 1999), 206-62.

5. For the link between Syriac wings language and the feminine gender of the Spirit see, Sebastian Brock, "The Holy Spirit as Feminine in Early Syriac Literature", in Janet M. Soskice (ed.), *After Eve: Women, Theology and the Christian Tradition* (London, Marshall Pickering, 1990), 73-87 and Susan Ashbrook Harvey, "Feminine Imagery for the Divine: The Holy Spirit, the Odes of Solomon and Early Syriac Tradition", *Saint Vladimir's Theological Quarterly* 37/ 2-8 (1993): 111-39.

6. S. A. Harvey, "Feminine Imagery for the Divine", 116.

charismata of the Holy Spirit, particularly with respect to nurturing and pedagogic aspects of sanctification. In several cases, the Spirit is referred to using the feminine grammatical gender, this is particularly in evidence when Macarian teaching links the mother Spirit with the heavenly Jerusalem. But more often the feminine Greek noun, 'grace' (ἡ χάρις) is used to express the beneficence and empowerment of the divine Spirit. This tendency is most clearly evident when the *Homilies* describe a mother bird, brooding, nurturing and teaching her chicks to fly and this is related analogically to the Christian's experience of the 'wings of the Spirit'. In such examples, which I shall further present in detail, ἡ χάρις seems to function as a Greek transliteration of the Syriac, *rûhâ* (spirit), and the influence of a Syriac symbolic thought-world and spirituality seem particularly obvious.

Following the foundational research of Hermann Dörries[7], there has been a growing scholarly consensus regarding the Syro-Mesopotamian context of the *Macriana* corpus. In 1964, Gilles Quispel and Dom A. Baker published papers demonstrating that Macarius quoted from a text of the Gospels related to the Syrian, *Gospel of Thomas* and *Diatessaron* group of witnesses.[8] Recent work by Columba Stewart on the *Homilies*, has highlighted the Syriac background to clothing, mixing, blending, filling and indwelling metaphors.[9] Robert Murray has tabulated the plethora of titles of Christ which the Macarian corpus shares with 2nd to 4th century Christian Syriac writings.[10] Alexander Golitzin has traced a set of Macarian "divine light" themes back to Ephrem the Syrian, the anonymous Syriac, *Book of* Steps, Aphrahat the Persian Sage and the context of *merkavah* mysticism in the Jewish Babylonian rabbinic schools.[11] Remarkably, this group of themes connecting, "the Glory of God, the liturgy of the angels, and Adamic splendour, set in the imagery and theology of the

7. H. Dörries, *Symeon von Mesopotamien. Die Überlieferung der messalianischen Makarios-Schrifte*, Texte und Untersuchungen 55/1 (Leipzig-Berlin, 1941).

8. A. Baker, "Pseudo-Macarius and the Gospel of Thomas", *Vigiliae Christianae* 18 (1964): 215-25, and Gilles Quispel, "The Syrian Thomas and the Syrian Macarius", *Vigiliae Christianae* 18 (1964): 226-35.

9. Columba Stewart, '*Working the Earth of the Heart': The Messalian Controversy in History, Texts and Language to AD 431*, Oxford Theological Monographs (Oxford, Clarendon Press, 1991), 169-233 & 285-301.

10. Robert Murray, *Symbols of Church and Kingdom: A Study in Early Syriac* Tradition (London, T & T Clark, revised edition, 2006), 354-63.

11. A. Golitzin, 'Recovering the "Glory of Adam": "Divine Light" Traditions in the Dead Sea Scrolls and the Christian Ascetical Literature of Fourth-Century Syro-Mesopotamia', in *The Dead Sea Scrolls as Background to Postbiblical Judaism and Early Christianity : Papers from an International Conference at St. Andrews in 2001*, ed. James R. Davila (Leiden, Brill, 2003), 275-308.

Temple and promising fellowship with heaven and the recovery of Paradise" (Golitzin), are paralleled by the teaching of Jewish covenanters from Qumran, at the turn of the era.[12]

While the Syrian background and context for the *Macarian* Homilies is now more widely accepted, the weight of scholarship continues to assert that the basic structure and teaching of Macarian pneumatology was influenced primarily by Greek dogmatic theology. In particular, that it reflected the Christian neo-Platonic Alexandrian tradition of Clement and Origen as then being interpreted and refined by the Cappadocian bishop theologians, the brothers Basil of Caesarea and Gregory of Nyssa and Basil's soul-friend, Gregory Nazianzen. In this conceptual framework, the language of wings in the *Macriana* has been universally assumed to reflect the same vestiges of the popular myth of the loss and regaining of the 'wings of the soul' from Plato's, *Phaedrus,* as the Christianized appropriation in the writings of the Cappadocian Fathers.[13] Since, to date, there has not been a recognition of possible links with an alternative Syriac tradition of wings language, this work must address two methodological issues.

Firstly, how to demonstrate clearly a Syriac influence. In Part I, my approach will be to describe the evolution and types of usage of 'wings of the Spirit' language in 4th century Syriac Christianity. Here, as well as presenting translated sources, I shall offer some commentary upon this treasury of inspirational poetry, hymnody and teaching. In Part II, I shall compare this Syriac Christian usage with thematic clusters in Macarian pneumatology. I shall then describe and examine one extended mother-bird-fledgling analogy in detail.

A second area for further discussion relates to wider issues of cultural and religious meaning in metaphorical language. In particular, the question as to how far there was a pan-Christian ethos based upon the language of the Bible and half a millennia of cultural convergence within the Greco-Roman Empire. Sebastian Brock argues that while it is legitimate to speak of two poles of religious discourse, analytical and philosophical in the Greek-speaking Eastern empire and symbolic, poetic and synthetic in the Syrian and Persian Orient, with the genre of religious imagery this distinction is often blurred.[14] For example, both Ephrem of Syria and Gregory

12. Ibid., 306. See also 207-9 & 305-7.

13. Plato, *Phaedrus* 245c-249d, ed. & English trans. R. Hackforth (Cambridge, 1952). For further discussion, see Part III, Chapter 8.

14. Sebastian Brock, *The Luminous Eye: The Spiritual World Vision of Saint Ephrem the Syrian*, Cistercian Study Series 124 (Kalamazoo, MI, 1992), 145-8.

of Nyssa used mirror imagery to describe how the vision of the inner eye of faith functions, both spoke of Christ as the heavenly Bridegroom, both employed the antinomies of light and darkness, beauty and ugliness.

In the light of this observation, it is legitimate to ask whether the Macarian usage of the evocative metaphor of the 'wings of the Spirit', with its roots in a Semitic Jewish-Christian religious tradition and practice, held pan-Christian appeal. It could be invoked to interpret the popular neo-Platonic Christian ethico-mystical ascent on the 'wings of the soul', to ascetics in the western Greek-speaking region of Syria around Antioch. Conversely, it may have been part of a linguistic mission to promote the Syrian enthusiasm for direct religious experience and prophecy to the beleaguered orthodox Church in the Eastern Roman Empire, wrestling with arguments over the divinity of the Holy Spirit.

In Part III of this short study, I hope to show that the Macarian metaphor of the 'wings of the Spirit', indeed functioned as an interpretative bridge between the Greek and Syriac cultural milieus of religious discourse and ascetic praxis. Whilst a Cappadocian influence upon Macarian pneumatology is evident, so is the converse. In the later ascetical and spiritual writings of Gregory of Nyssa, written in semi-retirement after the Ecumenical Council of Constantinople, (between AD 381-394), it is possible to find traces of Macarian influence, both in terms of ideas and literary dependence. I shall conclude this study with a discussion of Gregory's last homily in his mystical treatise, *Commentary on the Song*. I hope to illustrate that there was a cross fertilization of linguistic and symbolic worldviews between the Syrian elder and the Greek philosopher bishop, leading to a mutual enrichment of their respective ascetic and spiritual teachings on the wings of divinity.

PART I

'WINGS OF THE SPIRIT': EARLY SYRIAC SYMBOLIC PNEUMATOLOGY

CHAPTER 1

THE DESCENT OF THE 'HOVERING' WINGS OF THE SPIRIT IN THE SACRAMENTAL 'MYSTERIES'

'As the wings of the doves over their nestlings,
and the mouths of their nestlings towards their mouths,
so are the wings of the Spirit over my heart.
My heart continually refreshes itself and leaps for joy,
like the babe who leaps for joy in his mother's womb.'

Odes of Solomon 28:1-2.[1]

In this beautiful Syriac hymn, probably dating from the early 2nd century AD,[2] the Odist describes an ecstatic experience of the Holy Spirit in the imagery of a mother bird protectively flapping over and warming her chicks in the nest. The context for this religious experience was probably the initiation of baptism. This is hinted at in the hymn in two ways. The joyful leaping in the womb, reflects the Lukan story of the unborn baby, John the Baptist, leaping in Elisabeth's womb when she met Mary, pregnant with Jesus. In Syriac Christianity, baptism was understood in Johannine terms as a spiritual rebirth through the womb of the Spirit in the waters of baptism.[3] To prepare for this transformative event, initiates received pre-baptismal anointing, which was understood as 'signing' *(rûshmâ)* in oil by the Spirit.[4] Up to the early 4th century, they would also

1. *The Odes of Solomon*, critically edited & translated into English by James H. Charlesworth, 2nd edition (Missoula, 1977), 108-9.
2. Dating the *Odes* remains highly problematic. James H. Charlesworth and R. A. Culpepper argue for a 1st century date, see their, "The Odes of Solomon and the Gospel of John", *Catholic Biblical Quarterly* 35 (1973): 298-321. Han J.W. Drijvers has consistently pressed for a 3rd century date, see the relevant articles collected in his, *East of Antioch: Studies in Early Syriac Christianity* (London, Variorum, 1984). The generally accepted view is a 2nd century date , see B. McNeil, "The Odes of Solomon and the Scriptures", *Oriens Christianus* 67 (1983): 104-22.
3. John 3:3-7. S.A. Harvey, in *Feminine Imagery*, 119, contrasts the Syriac baptismal emphasis on birth imagery from John 3 v.3-6, with the usage in the Greco-Roman Church of the Pauline emphasis in Romans 6: 4-6 on dying and rising, which seemed to encourage the view that the baptismal water was a tomb. See for example, Basil of Caesarea, *On the Holy Spirit* 15.35.
4. Sebastian Brock, "The Syrian Baptismal Rites", *Concilium* 22(1979): 98-104 and G. Winkler, "The Original Meaning of the Pre-Baptismal Anointing and its Implications", *Worship* 52 (1978): 24-45.

have been required to have taken vows of either virginity, or if married, of sexual continence. The 'sons and daughters of the Covenant' continued this practice throughout the 4th century on a voluntary basis.[5] Their aim was to become a consecrated 'single one' (*îhîdayâ*), a term meaning celibate, solitary, single-minded (by accepting the 'circumcision of the heart') and Christ-like.[6] Descending under 'the wings of the Spirit', the baptismal candidate entered the water where s/he 'mingled' with the Spirit and 'put on' Christ. Thus restored to the primordial Adamic image through grace, s/he could re-enter Paradise and immortal life in fellowship with the angels and Christ, the heavenly 'Bridegroom' (*hathnâ*).

The descent of the Holy Spirit to sanctify the waters and regenerate children of God, was linked with an image of the Holy Spirit as a mother bird 'hovering' over her clutch or nestlings. While this metaphor may have been partly evoked by the Markan account of the descent of the dove at Christ's baptism, the archetypal biblical image for this unique Syriac interpretation was drawn from the *Peshitta* translation of Genesis 1:2b. Here the 'Spirit of God' is described 'hovering' (*rûhhafâ*) over the primeval waters. Eusebius bishop of Emesa, who was born in Edessa about 300 AD, discussed this verse in his Greek, *Commentary on the Octateuch and Reigns*. He argued that the Greek Septuagint translation: 'the Spirit of God was moving over the waters', failed to grasp the Hebrew meaning adequately and made an appeal to the *Peshitta* usage of *rûhhafâ*, which he claimed meant: ' "The Spirit was brooding", "it stirred", "it was moving over", like a bird that warms its young under its wings and at the same time strokes them with tenderness and by brooding on (them), while shifting about ...'[7]

The brooding and hovering imagery for the Spirit over the waters of creation and baptism are made explicit in several mid 4th century hymn-cycles in stanza forms (*madrashe*) attributed to Ephrem the Syrian. Ephrem was a leading deacon and *Rabban* (head of a catechetical school

5. Both Aphrahat and Ephrem, while acknowledging the goodness of marriage, chose to become *bnai qeiãmã*.

6. For a good summary of the scholarly reconstruction of early Syriac proto-monasticism and the role and function of the *îhîdãyâ* see S. Beggiani, *Introduction to Eastern Christian Spirituality: The Syriac Tradition* (London, Associates University Presses, 1991), 16-28 and Robert Murray, *Symbols of Church*, 3-17.

7. Eusebius of Emesa, Fragment III.1:2.40-43, English trans. R. Bas Ter Haar Romeny, *A Syrian in Greek Dress: The Use of Greek, Hebrew and Syriac Biblical Texts in Eusebius of Emesa' s Commentary on Genesis*, Traditio Exegetica Graeca 6 (Louvain, Peeters, 1997), 176.

of Christian exegesis) in the Roman Syrian frontier town of Nisibis on the River Euphrates. He was a prolific writer producing both commentaries and lyric poetry of such beauty and depth that his over four hundred hymns began to be translated into Greek at an early date. His hymns, crammed with biblical imagery and typology, comprised of complex patterns of syllabic rhythms and were set to melodies for use throughout the liturgical year.[8] They were sung in the church by a choir of consecrated women, whom Ephrem trained as choir master.

According to the Syriac poet, chorepiskopos Jacob of Serugh, Ephrem as a poet wrote specifically for women.

> 'The blessed Ephrem saw that the women were silent from praise
> and in his wisdom he decided that it was right that they should sing out;
> so just as Moses gave timbrels to the young girls,
> thus did this discerning man compose hymns for virgins'.[9]

In the following excerpt from Ephrem's, *Hymns on Epiphany*, a symbolic link is made between the dynamic mothering of creation by the hovering of the Spirit of God over the primeval waters and the birthing of Christians in the baptistery.

> 'In the beginning the Spirit brooded — hovered on the waters;
> they conceived and gave birth — to serpents and fishes and birds.
> The Holy Spirit has hovered in baptism,
> and in mystery has given birth to eagles, — virgins and bishops,
> and in mystery has given birth to fishes, — holy ones and intercessors;
> and in mystery to serpents, — lo! the wise have become simple as doves!'
>
> *Hymns for the Feast of Epiphany* 8:16.[10]

In these, *Hymns on Epiphany*, there are two direct references to the 'hovering' of the descending Spirit over the waters,[11] there is also a description of baptism itself as, 'spreading her wings'[12], and there is a play on the verb 'to hover' (*rahef*) which, when used of God, can also mean, to be compassionate or merciful.[13] It is therefore surprising that in his late, *Commentary on Genesis*, Ephrem refuted the association of the Hebrew word *ruach*, (spirit/wind/breath) in Genesis 1:2b with either the Spirit or a

8. For a description of Ephrem's poetic form, see, Sebastian Brock, *St. Ephrem the Syrian: Hymns of Paradise* (Crestwood, NY, St. Vladimir's Seminary Press, 1990), 36-39.
9. Jacob of Serugh, *Acta Martyrum et Sanctorum*, ed. P. Bedjan (Paris and Leipzig, 1892), 672. Cited by Sebastian Brock, *St. Ephrem the Syrian*, 23.
10. *H.Epiph.* 8.16 (CSCO 186, Syr. 82-3), 173, English trans. A.E. Johnston, in J. Gwynn, ed., *Nicene and Post-Nicene Fathers*, 13/2 2 (Oxford 1898; reprint Eerdmans, 1976), 278.
11. *H.Epiph.* 6.1 & 8.16, Johnston, 273 & 278.
12. *H.Epiph.* 9.2, Johnston, 279.
13. *H.Epiph.* 8.1, Johnston, 276.

mother bird.[14] This anomaly led Dom Edmund Beck, the editor of the new series of critical editions of Ephrem's works, to question the authorship of some of the *Epiphany Hymns.*[15]

There are other explanations for this shift in Ephrem's teaching. In 363 AD, the Romans handed Nisibis over to the Persians as part of a peace treaty. Ephrem and his Christian community were forced to migrate a hundred miles to the west, and settled in the cosmopolitan city of Edessa. Here, the local syncretistic cults of Mani and Bardaisan were still flourishing and Ephrem began to write polemical refutations of their doctrines. Edward Matthews has suggested that it was in this later struggle with Bardaisian teaching that Ephrem may have toned down the mothering aspect of the Spirit.[16]

A more plausible explanation has been offered by Brock, who has demonstrated that beginning around the year 400 AD, there was a definite shift in Syriac biblical translation techniques as the Antiochen School began to adjust and conform to Greek technical language for the dogmas.[17] In later versions of the New Testament, such as the early 5th century *Peshitta* and 7th century *Harklean*, the grammatically feminine name for the Spirit in the Old Syriac gradually became changed to masculine, although feminine 'hovering' language was retained in the liturgy. Jansma has reviewed the ensuing discussion about the interpretation of Genesis 1:2b amongst Syriac exegetes up until the 11th century.[18]

While the key Genesis etymology was open to debate, by the 4th Century, 'hovering' language had achieved an iconic status in connection with Syriac sacramental liturgical rites. The classic example of its usage for baptism was composed in 337 AD by Aphrahat the Persian Sage, a bishop of influence in Persian Babylonia.

> 'For by baptism we receive the Spirit of Christ, and at that moment when the priests invoke the Spirit, She opens the heavens and descends and hovers over the waters, and those who are baptized put Her on. For the Spirit is far

14. Ephrem, *Commentary on Genesis,* 7.1, English trans., E. Matthews, *St. Ephrem the Syrian: Selected Prose Works*, ed. K. McVey, Fathers of the Church (Washington, Catholic University of America Press, 1994), 78-9.

15. In E. Beck's critical edition of Ephrem' s hymn cycles (*madrashe*), in the *Corpus Scriptorum Christianorum Orientalium* (CSCO; Louvain: Peeters), he appended the *Hymns on the Epiphany* to the *Hymns on the Nativity,* with a discussion of their authenticity, see CSCO 186, vii-viii, 187, viii-xiii.

16. E. Matthews, *St. Ephrem the Syrian*, 60-63 and 79, fn 45.

17. Sebastian Brock, "The Holy Spirit as Feminine in Early Syriac Literature", 75-76.

18. T. Jansma, "Investigations into the Early Syrian Fathers on Genesis", in B. Gemser (ed.), *Studies on the Book of Genesis* (Leiden, Brill, 1958), vol. 12, 69-181.

> from all who are born of the body until they come to the birth from water, and then they receive the Holy Spirit'
>
> *Demonstration* 6:14[19]

Here, there is an obvious allusion to the baptism of Jesus in the River Jordan when the heavens were, "torn open" and the Spirit descended upon Jesus in the water (Mark 1:9-10). The Spirit's descent and hovering is understood as a divine initiative of blessing, consecration and sanctification. Her dynamic presence transforms the baptismal waters into the waters of the womb as she regenerates the Christian into a new subject whose life now depends upon the Spirit's mothering nurture and grace.

An important aspect of this teaching for this study is the fact that Aphrahat did not allude specifically to a dove, but rather to the dynamic movement of the bird-like wings of the Spirit. This accords with the Syriac interpretation of Genesis 1:2b but also highlights a significant element of this tradition, namely that the mother-bird imagery for the Holy Spirit had its roots in a plethora of associations from the Hebrew Scriptures including the protective wings of God in Psalmody and the maternal imagery for God in Isaiah.[20] Of particular significance is another usage of *rûhhafâ* in the *Peshitta*. Deuteronomy 32:11, describes the caring Presence of the Lord for the children of Israel during their exodus in the wilderness:

> 'Like an eagle that stirs up its nest,
> hovering over its young,
> spreading out its wings,
> bearing them on its pinions'.

Here, the emphasis is upon the protection, nurturing and bearing of the Israelites by the dynamism and empowerment of the divine wings.

Leander Keck, in her detailed study of the background to the dove imagery in the Markan account of the baptism of Jesus, has concluded that in its original Palestinian Jewish Aramaic Christian tradition, the emphasis was also on the movement and actions of the bird.[21] In her opinion, 'the Spirit coming with dove-like descent, became reified into a dove-like Spirit in the transmission of the gospel tradition to Hellenistic Christians'.[22] This shift was partly due to the ambiguous nature of Mark's

19. Aphrahat, *Demonstrationes* 6.14, ed. R. Graffin, *Patrologia Syriaca* (Paris, 1894), I, col. 292, 24-293.5. English trans. S. A. Harvey, *Feminine Imagery for the Divine*, 117.

20. See Robert Murray, *Symbols of Church and Kingdom*, 312-20.

21. Leander Keck, "The Spirit and the Dove", *New Testament Studies* 17 (1970-71): 41-67.

22. *Ibidem*, 63.

phrase, ὡς περιστεράν, which is both adverbial and adjectival because it originally represented the Hebrew word from Genesis 1:2b.

In the hymnody and writings of Ephrem the Syrian, references to the hovering of the Spirit can be gleaned from every aspect of the sacramental life of the Church. As well as in the context of baptism,[23] there are instances at ordination[24] and the Eucharist.[25] Seely Beggiani comments, 'In the Syriac mind, all acts of power and sanctification are the work of the Holy Spirit'.[26] In the rich symbolic world-view of Ephrem, where types and mysteries (*raza*) from Scripture and nature revealed the God 'clothed' in flesh, the sacraments played a central role. Here, through the Spirit as both agent and Gift, God 'mingled' with (*mzag*) or 'indwelt'/'took up residence in' (*shra*) the believing participant.

In Ephrem' s most important hymn on the nature and work of the Holy Spirit[27], communion with the Spirit through the Eucharist is described as a transformation into the angelic nature of fire and Spirit. (The Syriac usage of the term 'Watchers', *'îrê* for the heavenly angels, probably derived from the Jewish apocalyptic *'Book of the Watchers'*, I Enoch 1-34, written about 200 BC, and from Daniel.)[28]

> 'In your Bread is hidden a Spirit not to be eaten,
> in your Wine dwells a Fire not to be drunk.
> Spirit in your Bread, Fire in your Wine,
> a wonder set apart, [yet] received by our lips!
> When the Lord came down to earth, to mortals,
> a new creation he created them, like to the "Watchers".
> He mingled fire and spirit in them,
> to make them fire and spirit within.'
>
> *Hymns on Faith* 10:8-9.

23. *H.Epiph.* 6,1 (CSCO 186 Syr 82),160, *H.Fid.* 51,7 & 77,20; *H.Virg.*7,8.
24. Car.Nis. 19,2 (CSCO 218, Syr. 92), 50.
25. *H.Fid.*10, 16-17 (CSCO 154, Syr 73), 51. See E. Beck, "Die Eucharistie bei Ephräm", *Oriens Christianus* 38 (1954): 41-67, esp. 55-6 on 'hovering' and the Eucharist.
26. S. J. Beggiani, *Early Syriac Theology: With Special Reference to the Maronite Tradition* (London, University Press of America, 1983), 73.
27. *H.Fid.* 10 (CSCO 154, Syr 73), 51, English trans. Robert Murray, 'A Hymn of St Ephrem to Christ on the Incarnation, the Holy Spirit, and the Sacraments', *Eastern Churches Review* 3 (1970): 142-50.
28. For the theme of fellowship with the angels shared between Syrian asceticism and the Qumran literature, see Robert Murray, "Some Themes and Problems of Early Syriac Angelology", in R. Lavenant, *Symposium Syriacum* 1988, OCA 236 (Rome, Pontifical Institute of Oriental Studies, 1990), 143-53.

Later in the hymn, the Holy Spirit's hovering action of consecration over the altar cloth is related to the overshadowing of Mary at the Annunciation.

> 'See, Power concealed in the cloth of the sanctuary,
> a power which no mind has ever conceived.
> His love bent down, descended and hovered
> over the cloth on the altar of reconciliation.
> See, Fire and Spirit in the womb that bore you!'
>
> *Hymns on Faith* 10:16-17a.[29]

In Brock's discussion of this parallelism between the 'hovering' of the Spirit at the Incarnation and the priestly invocation of the Spirit at the Eucharist,[30] he refers to the famous set of five hymns where Ephrem meditated on the mystery of Christ the Pearl.[31] The widespread myth that when lightening struck an oyster, a pearl was formed as a conjunction of fire and water, is here a symbol both of the descent of the Spirit into Mary's womb and into the 'pearls' of the consecrated elements. In both cases, humanity 's receptive co-operation with the Holy Spirit leads to the divinization of the material world through grace. Characteristically, Ephrem described this transforming gift of sanctification in terms of flying to pre-lapsarian Paradise, the home of Adam and Eve before the Fall.

> 'The Spiritual Bread of the Eucharist : makes light and causes to fly:
> the Peoples have been wafted up : and have settled in Paradise.
> By means of the Spiritual Bread : everyone becomes
> an eagle who reaches : as far as Paradise.'
>
> *Hymns on Unleavened Bread* 17:8-12.

29. *H.Fid.*10: 16-17a., Robert Murray, *A Hymn of St. Ephrem*, 144.

30. Sebastian Brock, "Mary and the Eucharist: An Oriental Perspective", *Sobernost/ Eastern Churches Review* 1: 2 (1979): 50-9.

31. *Ibidem*, 56. The 'Hymns of the Pearl' are *H.Fid.* 81-85, English trans. by Sebastian Brock of Hymn 82 in his *Harp of the Spirit,* Studies Supplementary to Sobornost 4 (1975): 31-3.

CHAPTER 2

THE ASCENT ON WINGS IN SPIRITUAL STATES OF GRACE, INSPIRATION AND CONTEMPLATION

'Let us pray for the Holy Spirit to descend,
so that we may mingle Her within ourselves
and so fly to Heaven on Her wings.'

Hymns on the Church 21:1.[1]

The metaphors of wings and flying are characteristic of early Syriac devotional language, particularly in relation to exalted states of the mind, heart or spirit. In the above cited verse, Ephrem summed up his understanding of the divine economy of grace in terms of a reciprocal movement; through the Incarnation and the descent of the Spirit, Christians are raised up from the fallen state of Adam and lifted up to communion with God on the wings of the Spirit. In the *Hymns on Faith*, the life of a bird from egg to fledgling is used to symbolize this religious experience of a growing sense of faith, praise, love and truth.

'A chick not yet fully formed
in its weakness cannot break its shell;
so faith, held in silence, is likewise weak.
O perfect it, You who perfects all things!
A bird grows up in three stages,
from womb to egg, then to nest where it sings;
and once it is full grown it flies in the air,
opening its wings in the symbol of the Cross.

Truth and Love are wings that cannot be separated,
for Truth without Love is unable to fly,
so too Love without truth is unable to ascend:
their yoke is one of harmony.'

Hymns on Faith 18:1-2 & 6.[2]

In this analogy, the nestling has to learn to fly. There is a certain stress here upon the Christian's effort to mature in the faith and develop

1. Ephrem, *H.Eccl.*21:1 (CSCO 198), 46. Cited by Columba Stewart, '*Working the Earth of the Heart': The Messalian Controversy in History, Texts and language to AD 431*, Oxford Theological Monographs (Oxford, Clarendon Press, 1991), 194.
2. *H.Fid* 18: 1-2 & 6, English trans. Sebastian Brock, *The Luminous Eye*, 79 & 59.

Christ-like virtues. Ascent on the wings requires self-sacrifice in imitation of Christ, in Syriac, *msarrqûtâ* or self-stripping. Co-operation between freewill and the salvific grace of the Spirit is a central tenet of Ephrem's theology.

There is nevertheless in early Syriac pneumatology a deep sense of the charismatic and ecstatic gifts of the divine Spirit. A pertinent example for this study is from the late 4th century writer, Cyrillona. In his *memre* for Easter, he reflected on Christ's promise in John 14-16, to send the Paraclete.

'The Spirit will come with her tongues
and the Paraclete with his revelations.
A new speech will dwell in you;
the wings of the Spirit will be folded upon you,
they will fly [down] from on high
and they will dwell upon your mouths;
Upon your lips shall dwell the fire
and in your mouths the flame.'

On the Pasch. 158-159.[3]

The passage continues by comparing the Pentecostal *charismata* of tongues with the unconsumed fire in the burning bush and the 'tongues of the Spirit' which descending upon Mary's womb, brought forth 'the divine conception'. This dense typological symbolism highlights the intensely experiential nature of the Spirit's actions in the life of the Christian. A key Syriac term for the Holy Spirit was 'the Power' (*haylâ*); the encounter with the Spirit was considered an intimate but awesome mingling with the vivifying and perfecting energies of the divine *ruha*. As Helen Schüngel-Straumann points out in her study of the *rwh 'elohim* (Spirit of God) in Second Temple Judaism, the term meant both Spirit, breath and (storm) wind and signified the dynamic life-giving force of creative potentiality and energy. In this Semitic world-view, God's Spirit is both aspiration and aeration, and bound up with the speaking of God's creative Word.[4] In Cyrillona's meditation, the Spirit births a new form of communication based upon divine revelation. Like the Mother of God, the Apostles conceive the Word (*melltâ*) through the descent of the Spirit. They are then consecrated and empowered to proclaim the Gospel, to teach divine truth and to prophesy. These gifted forms of fiery speech are blessed and inspired by the wings of the Spirit, 'folded' over the mouths of the disciples.

3. *Hymni et Sermones*, Syr., ed. G. Bicknell, *ZDMG* 27 (1873): 579, English tr. Robert Murray, *Symbols*, 81.

4. Helen Schüngel-Straumann, *Rûah bewegt die Welt*, Stuttgarter Bibelstudien 151 (Stuttgart: Katholisches Bibelwerk, 1992), 83-4.

In both Aphrahat and Ephrem's writings, the related metaphor of the 'the wings of thought' seems to be associated with spiritual and intellectual modes of perception. At the beginning of his hymn cycle, *On Paradise*, Ephrem described the process of meditation which gave him insight into the meaning of the Genesis story of the Garden of Eden.

> 'My tongue read the story's: outward narrative,
> while my intellect took wing: and soared upward in awe
> as it perceived the splendour of Paradise: not indeed as it really is,
> but insofar as humanity: is granted to comprehend it.'
>
> *Hymns on Paradise* 1:3b.[5]

In Ephrem 's understanding of revelation, the unknowable 'hidden' God had graciously chosen to 'clothe' Himself in the 'names' of Scripture and in the flesh of Jesus for the benefit of human understanding and salvation. Through contemplation and the inspiration of the Spirit, the 'hidden power' of this divine symbolic language could be discerned. It is clear in this passage that the flight of thought is not simply a metaphor for natural intellectual activity but is a divine gift leading to illumination.

In Aphrahat's encyclical letter, written for the Council of Seleucia in 344, there is a remarkable passage describing the transformation of the perfected sage into the dwelling place of the Throne of God. The visionary experience begins with a search for Wisdom.

> 'The wings of the understanding are spread out,
> and the wings of thought are unfold,
> and the senses of the intellect are exploring,
> and the eyes of the conscience are exploring.'
>
> *Demonstration* 14[6]

Columba Stewart carefully demonstrates that Aphrahat used the phrases, 'senses of the mind', of the 'intellect', of 'thought', of 'intelligence' and of 'meditations' as synonymous terms for, 'spiritual and intellectual modes of apprehension'.[7] Further in this passage, Wisdom comes to dwell in the heart of the 'sage' (*hakimā*).

> 'In Her he possesses a hidden treasure. He flies in his thought to all the heights, and his ponderings descend to all the depths. She inscribes in his

5. *H.Parad.*1:3b, English trans. Sebastian Brock, as *St. Ephrem the Syrian: Hymns on Paradise* (New York, SVS Press, 1990), 78.

6. Aphrahat, *Demonstrationes* 14, ed. J. Parisot, *Patrologia Syriaca* (Paris, 1874), I. col. 660, 18-661.2, English trans., Columba Stewart, *Working the Earth of the Heart*, 165.

7. *Ibidem*, 165.

> heart a wondrous thing ... all things are enclosed within his thought, and his inclination to receive becomes still more vast: he becomes the great Temple of his Creator ...'
>
> *Demonstration* 14:35. [8]

The flight of illumination and vision inspired by God's Wisdom, is here described simultaneously as an ascent into the heavens and a descent into the heart, which is both the centre of the person of the sage and the dwelling place of 'the King of Heaven'. Golitzen has discussed this religious experience in the light of a similar emphasis on the interiorisation of the apocalyptic ascent in the *Macarian Homilies*. This important observation will be examined in the next section.

The use of wings language to describe religious and intellectual experiences of enlightenment raises the issue of Syriac anthropology. Was the human intellectual spirit (*tar'itha*), as the highest aspect of the tripartite body-soul-spirit, naturally winged? In other words, did it have some affinity with the angelic or divine nature? It would seem from these examples that it did have the God-given capacity to become winged when indwelt and illumined by the Holy Spirit. In Syriac Christianity this potential was linked to the recovery of the pre-fallen Adamic likeness in baptism and its realisation at the final resurrection of the dead.

In Aphrahat' *Demonstration* 6, *On the Sons of the Covenant*, which is considered one of the most important texts of Syrian proto-monasticism,[9] there is teaching on a two-stage resurrection. In the first stage at baptism, the Christian is reborn and 'puts on' the Spirit of Christ who dwells in the temple of the body and transforms it, 'into the likeness of the heavenly Adam' .... 'For the animal shall be swallowed up in the spiritual'. This rite of regeneration and possession by the Spirit requires the full assent and co-operation of the believer. If prayerful vigilance and righteous living is not maintained, the Holy Spirit is 'grieved'; the Christian can be 'stripped' of his/her spiritual nature and will have an animal nature at the resurrection. At death, the Spirit returns to heaven but at the general resurrection is reunited to the body which it reawakens,

8. *Demonstrationes* 14:35 (*P.S.* I, col. 661, 8-664:10), English trans. A. Golitzin, "Recovering the 'Glory of Adam'", 295-6.

9. See G. Nedungatt, "The Covenanters of the Early Syriac-Speaking Church", *Orientalia Christiana Periodica* 39 (1973): 191-215, 419-44 and Robert Murray, "The Exhortation to Candidates for Ascetical Vows at Baptism in the Ancient Syrian Church", *New Testament Studies* 21 (1974-5): 59-80.

reanimates and spiritually transfigures: 'And the Spirit which they have put on shall cause them to fly'.[10]

Aphrahat concluded:

> 'And death shall be swallowed up in life (1 Corinthians 15:54) and the body shall be swallowed up in Spirit. And by the power of the Spirit, that man shall fly up to meet the King and He shall receive him with joy, and Christ shall give thanks for the body that has kept His Spirit in purity'.[11]

The metaphor of flying in this passage is clearly linked to the supernatural work of the Holy Spirit and shows no hint of the 'wings of the soul' terminology from noetic Platonism. Beggiani claims, 'Aphrahat represents Syriac-speaking Christianity in its purest form, virtually uncontaminated by Greek influence'.[12] This is also affirmed by Jacob Neusner in his detailed study of Aphrahat's relationship to Babylonian Judaism.[13] The unique combination of an interpretation of the Pauline metaphors of 'putting on' or 'clothing' in the Spirit of Christ with eschatological hopes of a flight to heaven, derived from traditions of exegesis and imagery from intertestamental literature (*pseudepigrapha*) stretching back over centuries from the Syrian Orient to the Palestinian homeland of sectarian Jewish and Judeo-Christian migrants.[14]

In Ephrem' s eschatology, the 'putting on' of a spiritual raiment, the 'robe of glory,' was used to symbolise a process of sanctification and glorification through the Spirit which was also linked with the capacity to fly. This is presented as a schema of salvation in the poetry of his *Hymns on Paradise*. In primordial Paradise, Adam was created with the potential for immortality and full knowledge of God.[15] This divine intention was symbolised by Adam's promised high-priestly vestment, the 'robe of glory'.

10. *Demonstratione* 6:18, *Patrologia Syriaca* I, col. 308:1-13), English trans. J. Gwynn, Select Library of Nicene and Post Nicene Fathers, 2nd series, 13/ 3 (new edition, Grand Rapids, Eerdmans, 1976), 374.

11. Aphrahat, *Demonstratione* 6:18, English trans., Gwynn, 372.

12. S. Beggiani, *Introduction to Eastern Christian Spirituality*, 17.

13. Jakob Neusner, *Aphrahat and Judaism: The Christian- Jewish Argument in Fourth-Century Iran*, Studia Post-Biblica (Leiden, Brill, 1971). Neusner claims that Aphrahat had never even heard of Arius, see page 8.

14. That Syriac Christianity was part of a complex development of various Judeo-Christian sects from 1st or early 2nd century Palestine has become established scholarship as documents from Qumran, Nag Hammadi, and the *Cologne Mani Codex* have significantly added to our knowledge. See Robert Murray, "Disaffected Judaism and Early Christianity: Some Predisposing Factors", in *To See Us as Others See Us* (Chico, Scholars Press, 1985), 263-281 and Sebastian Brock, "Jewish Traditions in Syriac Sources", *JJS* 30 (1979): 212-32.

15. *H. Parad.* 3: 6-16 (CSCO 174), 10-12, English trans. Sebastian Brock, *Hymns on Paradise*, 92-6.

When, through disobedience to the commandments of God, Adam lost the hope of entering into the Holy of Holies, he degraded into an animal clothed only in skins and leaves.

Brock has demonstrated that according to Ephrem' s teaching, the Christian by 'putting on' Christ the Second Adam in the waters of baptism, received back by grace the promised 'robe of glory'. This renewed nature, effected through the Spirit, opened up again the potential for an angelic life of 'fire and Spirit' and the return to an eschatological Paradise.[16] At the resurrection of the dead, the righteous, robed in light, shall be wholly healed and restored. In the blessedness of their transfigured body-soul-spirit they shall fly in the divine Presence on the 'heights' of Paradise Mountain.

> 'Far more glorious than the body is the soul,
> and more glorious still than the soul is the spirit,
> but more hidden than the spirit is the Godhead.
> At the end the body will put on
> the beauty of the soul, the soul will put on that of the spirit,
> while the spirit shall put on the very likeness of God's majesty.
>
> For bodies shall be raised to the level of souls,
> and the soul to that of the spirit,
> while the spirit will be raised to the height of God's Majesty;
> clinging to both awe and love,
> it neither circles too high, nor holds back too much,
> it discerns when to hold back, so that its flight is beneficial.'
>
> *Hymns on Paradise* 9:19-20.[17]

16. Sebastian Brock, "Clothing Metaphors as a means of Theological Expression in Syriac Tradition", in Sebastian Brock, *Studies in Syriac Christianity: History, Literature and Theology*, Variorum Collected Studies Series (Hampshire, Ashgate, 1992), 12-20.

17. *H. Parad.* 9: 19-20 (CSCO 174), 34, English trans. Sebastian Brock, *Hymns on Paradise*, 143.

PART II

MACARIAN 'WINGS LANGUAGE': CONTEXT AND HERMENEUTICS

CHAPTER 3

MACARIUS-SYMEON, THE TEACHER OF HEART-FELT PRAYER AND ASCETIC PURIFICATION

The spiritual teacher, given the epithet, 'Makarios'- 'the Blessed One', was probably Symeon of Mesopotamia,[1] who is first mentioned by the historian Theodoret in connection with those leaders of the charismatic Messalian 'tendency'[2] who were condemned at the Synod of Side in 390 AD.[3] His writings include an encyclical treatise, the *Great Letter*[4], which Marcus Plested calls 'a kind of manifesto' advocating a vision for an authentic monasticism based upon inward religious experience.[5] Since the letter was addressed to 'Christian brothers' (the Macarian term for ascetic covenanters) and their spiritual elders, it can be assumed that the writer was a teacher of eminence and authority who was connected with a loose network of fraternal communities.[6] The consensus in scholarship today is that their context was of Syro-Mesopotamian provenance, but given that Macarius and presumably his disciples, were Greek-speaking, their location must have been in Roman Syria, west of the River Euphrates.[7] John

1. H. Dörries first identified the author of the Macarian corpus with Symeon of Mesopotamia in his, *Symeon von Mesopotamien*: see fn. 5. This view is shared by the German editors of the Macarian Collections and *Epistola Magna*.

2. Marcus Plested argues that Messalianism was not an organised movement but rather a radical charismatic 'tendency' within the Syrian Orient which spread west via Antioch. See his *The Macarian Legacy: The Place of Macarius-Symeon in the Eastern Christian Tradition*, Oxford Theological Monographs (Oxford, 2004), 16-27.

3. Theodoret, *Ecclesiastical History*, GCS 44, 229-31. Written around AD 440s.

4. The *Great Letter* or *Epistola Magna* (*EM*) is *Logos* 1 of Collection I and has been separately edited by W. Jaeger (Leiden, 1954) and more recently, using a wider manuscript base, by R. Staats as, *Makarios-Symeon: Epistola Magna. Eine messalianische Mönchsregel und ihre Umschrift in Gregors von Nyssa 'De Instituto Christiano'* (Göttingen, 1984).

5. M. Plested, *The Macarian Legacy*, 51.

6. *Epistola Magna*, Chapters 6-11 focus on the regulation of a community life in which service and prayer are complementary and guidance is given by 'elders' (προεστῶτες). Maloney describes it as, 'a very loose monastic organization with the prime accent on the development of interior humility and purity of heart to gain incessant prayer.', See, G. A. Maloney, *Pseudo-Macarius: The Fifty Spiritual Homilies and the Great Letter* (New York, Paulist Press, 1992), 251.

7. In the 4th century, Greek was the spoken and literary language in Roman Syria, west of the River Euphrates, see S. Brock, "Greek and Syriac in Late Antique Syria", in A.K. Bowman & G. Woolf (eds.), *Literacy and Power in the Ancient World* (Cambridge, Cambridge Univ. Press, 1994), 149-60.

McGuckin has suggested the region between Antioch and the churches of eastern Anatolia.[8]

The bulk of Macarian teaching exists in 'collections' of sayings (λόγοι) and sermons (ὁμιλία) which exist in four Byzantine medieval versions of the *Macarian Homilies.*[9] They are short allegories, analogies drawn from the worlds of nature, home-life and society, vivid similes, parables and moral teaching, sometimes in question and answer format. These include graphic personal descriptions of the interior life of spiritual warfare, prayer and 'mystical communion' (μυστική κοινωνία) with Christ the heavenly Bridegroom, through the indwelling Holy Spirit, the heavenly Mother and perfecter of the soul. As such they offered profound existential and psychological insight into the processes of purification and sanctification effected in the 'heart' by divine grace. The sayings were probably taught to disciples on a daily basis and thereafter collected, edited and circulated around a network of Syrian fraternal communities.[10]

The main themes in the *Macarian Homilies*, are quite repetitive but with an unusual and innovative vocabulary which stretched certain Greek words beyond their accepted meanings. Stewart has shown that the three key terms used, often in combination, to describe religious experience; πληροφορία for spiritual plenitude, αἴσθησις for spiritual sensation, and πεῖρα for spiritual experiences, had a peculiar Macarian meaning without direct Greek or Syriac precedence.[11] This is a significant observation for this study. Macarian teaching offered a new development in the history of eastern Christianity, namely a phenomenology of religious experience. In Plested's view, Macarius drew from both the Syriac symbolic paradigm based upon 'the Creator-creation distinction' and to a lesser degree,

8. J.A. McGuckin, *Standing in God's Holy Fire: The Byzantine Tradition*, Traditions of Christian Spirituality Series (London, Darton, Longman and Todd, 2001), 66.

9. Three collections have appeared in critical editions. Collection I was published in, *Makarios/Symeon: Reden und Briefe. Die Sammlung I des Vaticanus Graecus 694 (B)*, 2 vols., ed. H. Berthold (Berlin, Akademie-Verlag, 1973). Collection II appeared in, *Die 50 Geistlichen Homilien des Makarios, ed. H. Dörries, E. Klostermann 7 M. Kroeger*, PTS 4 (Berlin, de Gruyter, 1964). For an English translation of II see, G.A. Maloney, *Pseudo-Macarius: The Fifty Spiritual Homilies and the Great Letter* (N.Y., Paulist Press, 1992). Collection III appeared in *Neue Homilien des Makarios/Symeon aus Typus III*, ed. E. Klostermann & H. Berthold, TU 72 (Berlin, Akademie-Verlag, 1961). For the French translation with facing Greek text, *Pseudo-Macaire. Oeuvres spirituelles. Vol.I: Homélies propres á la Collection III*, ed. V. Desprez, SC 275 (Paris, Cerf, 1980). References to the *Macarian Homilies* begin with an uppercase Roman numeral designating the Collection, followed by Arabic numerals to designate a specific homily and subsection.

10. V. Desprez, *Pseudo-Macaire*, 28.

11. Columba Stewart, *Working the Earth of the Heart*, 96-168.

a 'noetic-sensible framework' closer to the Cappadocian usage of the Alexandrian allegorical tradition.[12] I would add that in neither case was he simply translating religio-cultural heritages. As a wordsmith, Macarius forged a new vocabulary for heart-felt spiritual teaching.

This study is concerned to demonstrate that Macarian teaching on the 'wings of the Spirit' was not simply a wholesale appropriation of the Origenist-Cappadocian usage of the Platonic vocabulary of the 'wings of the soul'. Rather the teaching drew upon a rich Syriac tradition which was then profoundly crafted by insights from personal religious experience and certain aspects of Cappadocian pneumatology. For the sake of clarity, I shall first explore possible parallels with the Syriac tradition described in Part I and discuss the relationship with Gregory of Nyssa's later writings in the final part. Since the frequent Macarian metaphor of the 'wings of the Spirit' is often linked with a wider set of maternal imagery for the Holy Spirit, it is necessary to first bed the teaching in this wider context before examining the main usages in thematic clusters.

12. M. Plested, *The Macarian Legacy*, 30.

CHAPTER 4

THE HOLY SPIRIT AS THE HEAVENLY MOTHER OF GRACE

Ἡ χρηστὴ καὶ οὐράνιος μήτηρ ἡ χάρις τοῦ πνεύματος

The maternal nature of the Holy Spirit in the *Macarian Homilies*, is a fundamental aspect of the ascetic Christian's relationship with the Divine. For the Syrian ascetics, 'born of the womb of the Spirit of the Godhead' [1], who had chosen celibacy and exile, the Holy Spirit replaced their earthly mothers as a beneficent source of comfort, nurture and formation.

> 'It is right and fitting, children, for you to have left all that is temporal and to have gone off to God: instead of an earthly father you are seeking the heavenly Father, and instead of a mother who is subject to corruption, you have as a Mother the excellent Spirit of God and the heavenly Jerusalem. Instead of brothers you have left, you now have the Lord who has allowed Himself to be called brother to the faithful.'
>
> *Macarian Homilies* I.54, 4.5.[2]

This passage while clearly reflecting a Syriac pneumatological background in general, links specifically with two teachings. In Aphrahat 's *Demonstration* 18:10, there is a *midrash* on Genesis 2:24 (where Adam is described leaving his mother to 'cleave' to a wife). Aphrahat commented: 'When a man has not yet taken a wife, he loves and honours God, his Father, and the Holy Spirit, his Mother and has no other love ... so also a man who has not yet taken a wife but remains solitary (*îhidâyâ*) is in one Spirit and one thought with his Father'.[3] In this example from Syriac proto-monasticism, celibacy is inextricably linked with a solitary life in which radical spiritual dependence on the Holy Spirit as Mother is a prerequisite for a profoundly focused life of prayer and virtue.

In a similar vein, in the Macarian corpus, 'single-mindedness', (*monotropos*), in faith and life-style, is a key Macarian virtue related to ἀπαθεία.[4] Single-mindedness meant, in purity of mind, body and soul, following the

1. II. 30, 2. E. trans., G. Maloney, 191.
2. I.54,4.5, ed. H. Berthold, vol. 2, 156-7.
3. *Demonstrationes*_18, 10a & 11b, English trans., J. Neusner, 82.
4. See G. Maloney, *Pseudo-Macarius*, 287, fn 7.

'narrow path' of imitating Christ in union with His indwelling Spirit of grace. For Macarius: 'Such a one, that is, who lives in the fellowship of only the divine Spouse, is totally simple in his single-mindedness.'[5]

The second significant link between the above mentioned passage and the Syriac tradition, is the association of the 'heavenly Jerusalem' or the 'heavenly Mother' with the Holy Spirit. There are several references in the *Homilies*, some of which cite the Pauline teaching on 'Jerusalem above' who is 'our mother' (Galatians 4:26). For example, Macarius identified: 'Jerusalem, the heavenly mother' with 'Rachel, the true mother, the heavenly grace, the Holy Spirit.'[6] The Pauline phrase was part of his discussion on the heritage of the heavenly Church for freeborn Christians. In early Greek Christianity it had led by an association of texts to the evolution of an ecclesiology of the motherhood of the Church.[7] In the Syriac trajectory, where the Holy Spirit was considered to be the mother of Christians, there seems to have been the development of a pneuma-ecclesiology in the late Fourth Century.

An important example of this evolution is mentioned by Robert Murray. He has demonstrated that in the 12th discourse of the anonymous Syriac, *Book of Steps*[8], there is, 'a whole systematic theology of the Church at three levels.'[9] While there is the public and 'visible' church with its ministry, sacramental life and service, there is also concurrently a 'hidden' or 'secret' church of the heart, and a heavenly church 'above'. The visible church, through the indwelling of the Spirit, acts as a mother to the, 'just' providing spiritual milk, but to the 'perfect' who, 'make their bodies temples and their hearts altars', the Spirit feeds the, 'solid food' of Christ and unites them with the heavenly church.[10]

The significant parallels with Macarian teaching suggest a common ethos and terminology. [11] Here too, the 'perfect' nurture a hidden church

5. *The Great Letter*, English trans., G. Maloney, 257.

6. I.61,2.1 & III.26. For references to the Holy Spirit as the 'heavenly mother' see also I. 54, 4.5; III.16, 2.3; III. 27. 1.2; III. 27. 4.2-3.

7. For example, in Origen's *Commentary and Homilies on the Song of Songs.*

8. R.A. Kitchen & M.F.G. Parmentier, in their introduction and new English translation, advocate a mid to late 4th century dating in Persian provenance. See Idem, *The Book of Steps: The Syriac Liber Graduum*, Cistercian Study Series 196 (Michigan, Cistercian Pub., 2004), xlix-lxi.

9. Robert Murray, *Symbols of Church*, 263. Murray offered his own English translation of Discourse 12, *On the Hidden and the Visible Ministry of the Church*, see, 264-68.

10. *Ibidem*, 265-7. The feeding with milk and meat reflects the Biblical teaching in 1 Corinthians 3:1-3 and Hebrews 5:12-14.

11. Earlier scholarship considered this ethos to be 'Messalian'. This is now considered a label without verifiable content and interest has shifted to the proto-monastic context of Syriac Christianity. For a good review of the debate, see Kitchen & Parmentier, *The Book of Steps*, xxi-xxvi & lxxxii-lxxxiii.

of the heart or soul,[12] which is an interior spiritual dimension to the visible life of the public church, and there are numerous exhortations to strive ascetically to enter the heavenly Church, a goal which can be partly realised in this earthly life.[13]

Of particular significance for this study is the shared emphasis upon the maternal functions of the Holy Spirit as She unites, sanctifies and ministers to the three levels of the Church. In the *Macarian Homilies*, this imagery is explored in a series of beautiful analogies. There are five which describe a divine Mother-Christian child relationship.[14] The emphasis throughout is upon the personal relationship between, 'the children of God who are begotten of the Holy Spirit through the Spirit's power'[15] and the loving care of the Divine. The maternal Spirit is described comforting her newborn baby, suckling it with milk from her breast.[16] She cuddles her infant[17] and when it falls over and cries, with loving pity she picks it up and nurses it.[18] She teaches it to talk in her own mother-tongue[19] and gradually weans it from milk to solid food.[20]

In three other examples, this intimate relationship between the gracious mothering of the Holy Spirit and her vulnerable Christian infant, is described in the imagery of a mother-bird-chick relationship.[21] In these 'parables' (παραβολαῖς)[22], the emphasis is upon the nestling growing and learning to fledge through the attentive care and training of the mother bird. In this teaching, the 'wings of the Spirit' play a key role. In the following example, I offer my own translation and précis of an extended analogy from *Collection* III. 16. 2,2-2,5.[23]

12. For example, I. 52.1.1-2; II.12.15 and II. 37. 8.
13. For example, II. 15. 25; II. 25.7; II.32. 2-3; II.44.4.
14. II. 46, 3; III. 22. 3.3; III. 27. 1.2: III. 27. 3.1; III. 27. 4. 2-3.
15. III. 2. 3 see also I.18. 5. 6.
16. III. 27.3.1 & III. 27. 4. 2-3.
17. III. 22, 3,3.
18. II. 46,3.
19. III. 27, 1,2.
20. III. 16, 2,2.
21. I. 3.6.1-4.; III.16.1. 2-3, 2,1 & 4-5; III.274.1.
22. The Macarian term for his usage of comparisons or allegories drawn from the natural world or Scripture. See, III. 16,3,1, ed. Desprez, 186, for his exposition of this didactic method which closely resembles the symbolic theology of Ephrem the Syrian.
23. Ed. Desprez, 183-86.

CHAPTER 5

THE PARABLE OF THE MOTHER-BIRD AND HER FLEDGLINGS

'Certain birds, fearing animals on the ground, such as rodents, build their home in a secluded place on a rooftop or high in a tree. The mother bird flies here and there bringing her nestlings the delicate nourishment which they are able to digest when they are small. Then, at the right time, she brings them more solid food in proportion to their stage of development, and at the same time she begins to teach them little by little to practise flying, and she trains them. First of all, around the nest, then around the branches of the tree they fly from branch to branch. Then they go a little further away. Finally, they reach adult maturity and their wings are fully developed. From then on they fly away with ease from hill to hill and from mountain to mountain. And so it is for the children of God who are born of the Holy Spirit through its power. First of all, in the beginning, hearts are fed with spiritual milk which is full of gentleness and heavenly affection (citations from I Cor. 3:2 and I Peter 2:2). Afterwards, gradually in proportion to progress in the growth and renewal of the soul, they are given more solid food and at the same time, 'the wings of grace' (τῆς χάριτος πτέρυγες)--that is to say, the power of the Spirit grows in the soul along with progress in good works. Following this, 'divine grace, the good and heavenly mother' (ἡ θεία χάρις ἡ ἀγάθη καὶ ἐπουράνιος μήτηρ) teaches the intellect to fly- first of all around the nest of the heart or the thoughts, that is to pray to God without distractions through spiritual power. Next, as the nourishment received from the divine Spirit becomes more solid, the soul is able to fly higher, guided and sustained through the Spirit. And finally the time of profit.

Once attained to the stature of the spiritual age (Ephesians 4:13), the intellect flies away with ease from hill to hill and from mountain to mountain. That is to say, from this world here to the world above and from this age now to the blessed age which is imperishable and infinite and with great 'freedom from care' (ἀμεριμνεσία) and 'rest' (ἀνάπαυσις). 'It is borne and guided by the wings of the Spirit towards visions and revelations of the heavenly mysteries, towards those ineffable 'spiritual contemplations' (θεορίας πνευματικάς) which the language of flesh cannot express.'

'At last, the children of God outgrow vice and are raised above it; fortified by the Spirit and having the skies for their abode, they no longer fear the ferocity of unclean spirits. Just as when birds mature; for once they are fully fledged, they no longer fear attacks either from beasts or man since for the most of the time, their sojourn is aerial. And just as there are individuals who do not know the habits of birds, so there are men filled with the spirit of this world who cannot understand the language of the Spirit; only the sons of the Spirit of grace know the language of their mother (1 Corinthians 2:13-14).'

In his commentary on his critical edition of *Collection* III., Vincent Desprez describes this analogy as the Macarian homily which most often treats the Spirit as the principle of action in prayer.[1] He suggests that the term, ἡ χάρις (grace), is used to describe the omnipresent, 'caractère maternel de Dieu' and reflects a Syrian background.[2] In his opinion, Macarius particularly used the term 'grace' in connection with the radical conversion of a person from the world and the devil to a life of humble submission to the will and commandments of God. 'Cette recréation est la nouvelle naissance, don de l'Esprit-Saint'.[3] However, Desprez assumes that the framework for this ascetic spirituality derived from the Cappadocians who provided, 'une structure souple mais ferme'.[4] In particular, that the ascent towards God, on 'the wings of the soul' was 'borrowed' from Gregory of Nyssa's appropriation of the Platonic myth of the wings of the soul from the *Phaedrus*, particularly in his, *Commentary of the Song*.[5]

In this study, I wish to challenge these last assumptions. I hope to demonstrate that while influenced by Gregory's heritage, the neo-Platonic Alexandrian tradition of Christian exegesis, Macarius taught from an independent Syriac tradition of teaching on the Holy Spirit. He innovatively and creatively shaped this pneumatology to the needs of his disciples. It is noteworthy that the Macarian vocabulary does not include the term, 'wings of the soul', but frequently uses phrases such as 'the wings of the Spirit' (τῶν πτέρυγων τοῦ πνεύματος) 'wings of the Holy Spirit' (πνεύματος ἁγίου πτέρυγας) or 'the wings of our mother' (τὰς πτέρυγας τῆς μητρὸς ἡμῶν). This usage clearly emphasises the divine initiative and support of the Holy Spirit rather than the free choice of the Christian to

1. V. Desprez, *Pseudo-Macaire*, 181, fn 2.
2. *Ibidem*, 325, fn 1.
3. *Ibidem*, 60, fn 5.
4. *Ibidem*, 47.
5. *Ibidem*, 58, fn13-14 & 180, fn1. See my discussion of this thesis in Part 3.

ascend to the Good and the Beautiful through the courageous struggle of virtue and intellection. In the balance of co-operation (*synergeia*) between human effort to conquer sin and divine grace to purify the heart, grace is the effective gift, the power and the goal.

While the Macarian usage of the 'wings of the Spirit' metaphor occurs, in my estimate, over twenty-five times, there is no specific attempt to interpret 'hovering' language into Greek. Probably the reason is that this ritual terminology was specifically evoked in the Syriac sacramental liturgical actions. In the *Macriana*, the sacraments of the 'visible Church' are acknowledged only rarely.[6] The main emphasis is upon the interior experience of 'the inner man' on his/her spiritual journey from 'baptism in fire and Spirit' to the maturity of 'the perfect measure (τέλειον μέτρον) of the fullness of Christ' (Ephesians 4:13). Nevertheless, the fact that the 'wings of the Spirit' metaphor is frequently associated with references to rebirth through the mother Spirit, demonstrates clearly both the link with Syrian baptism and the creative Macarian project to explore the psychology of the soul using familiar imagery. In my opinion, it cannot be a coincidence that to illustrate new life in the Spirit, analogies of mother-birds with their fledglings were drawn. The association of 'signing' in the Spirit, baptism in the womb of the Spirit and the invocation of the Spirit at the Eucharistic epiclesis, with the metaphor of the dynamic wings of a mother-bird from the creation story in Gen 1:2b, was deep-seated in the psyche of Syriac Christians.

'The Parable of the Mother-bird and her Fledglings' summarises the four main aspects of teaching on the 'wings of the Spirit' in the *Macarian Homilies*. These themes relate to the salvific power of the Spirit, divine aid and good works, protection and escape from enemies, and empowerment and illumination in prayer. These thematic clusters will now be briefly described with reference to their possible Syriac influences.

6. There are a few references to sacramental baptism, e.g.: I.43; I.52.1.4-5; II. 26, 23; II. 47.1; III.1.2.1; and the Eucharist, I.52.1.4.; I. 52.2.2-3.

CHAPTER 6

FOUR THEMATIC CLUSTERS OF TEACHING

A. The Wings of the Spirit Symbolize the Salvific Power (ΔΥΝΑΜΙΣ) of Divine Grace

Kallistos Ware succinctly describes the Macarian schema of salvation as a spiritual journey in 'three main stages'.[1] Initially, 'the heart is under the dominion of evil' which is so deeply ingrained that it cannot be overcome, 'without the assistance of divine grace'. Next follows a period of spiritual struggle between sin and grace simultaneously indwelling in the heart. Finally, sin is cast out from the heart, 'by the Holy Spirit, working in cooperation with the human will and the soul is united to Christ the heavenly Bridegroom and is "mixed" or "mingled" with the divine Spirit.' At every stage on this rite of passage from death to eternal life, the Holy Spirit as both the initiator and perfecter of salvation, is the divine principle of action. As shown above in the parable of 'The Mother-Bird and Her Fledglings', this dynamic Presence is specifically linked with, 'the wings of grace — that is to say, the power of the Spirit'.[2]

Macarius illustrated this teaching on salvific power using the language of wings in various ways. In a typological interpretation of the Mosaic Law, he described the priestly Levitical tradition of sacrificing one dove, then sprinkling a second with its blood and letting it fly free (Leviticus 14:4,22).

> 'But that which was done was a figure and shadow of the truth. For Christ was sacrificed and his blood, sprinkling us, made us grow wings. For he gave us the wings of the Holy Spirit to fly unencumbered into the air of the Godhead.'[3]

This Christological exegesis may have links with Ephrem' s teaching that the true offering of birds in Judaism was fulfilled in the incarnation and resurrection of Christ — His coming down and going up as a bird.[4] The imagery of flying to heaven on the wings of the Spirit, as earlier illustrated, was a common feature of Syriac devotional and eschatological writings. The ascent

1. K. Ware, 'Preface' to *Pseudo-Macarius*, ed. G.A. Maloney, xiii.
2. III. 16.2.3.
3. I. 11.1.2; II 47.2; IV. 12 Codex X; Maloney, 233.
4. *H.Nat.* 26:13., English trans., K.E. McVey, *Ephrem the Syrian: Hymns*, Classics of Western Spirituality (New York, Paulist Press, 1989), 209. See also fn 593.

to heaven on the wings of a sacrificial dove however, has its closest parallel in the Jewish *Apocalypse of Abraham*, when the Patriarch and an angel ascend to the heavenly temple on the wings of the two doves that Abraham had sacrificed to God on Mount Horeb. Martha Himmelfarb observes that this Jewish apocalypse underwent 'revision by Christians in the course of its transmission'.[5] For example, in chapter 29, Jesus is mentioned replacing the earthly temple in Jerusalem, destroyed by the Romans.[6]

This raises again the question Alexander Golitzin has posed about the context of Macarian spirituality. To what extent was it influenced by both the Jewish apocalyptic *hekhalot* vision of ascent to heaven in the 3 *Books of Enoch* and by Babylonian rabbinic *merkavah* mysticism focused on the divine chariot-throne of God?[7] While these questions cannot be fully addressed in this study, they are clearly significant. Is the ascent on the 'wings of the Spirit' modelled on a Platonic ascent of the soul or on the apocalyptic tradition in post-biblical Judaism of a sage's ascent to heaven? Or more specifically, as in Aphrahat's vision in his *Demonstration* 14, is that ascent an interiorization of the vision of God's temple and chariot-throne, inspired by the indwelling Holy Spirit? Golitzin argues that this is indeed the case in the Macarian allegory of Ezekiel's vision of the *merkavah*,[8] which I shall explore later in this chapter.

In *Homily* II.44.5-8, there is a collection of nautical similes illustrating the teaching that, 'our souls must be changed and transformed from the present state to a new one, to a divine nature' and thus, 'restored to the heavenly kingdom'.[9] This recreation is effected by, 'the power of the Holy Spirit'.[10] The Spirit, 'dredges up' the soul 'sunk into the waters of evil' and lightens its weight so it can, 'take up wings to the heights of Heaven'. Christ the Pilot, steers His crew over 'the bitter sea of sin and the dangerous abyss of the evil powers', in a boat which is compared to 'the buoyant and heavenly and winged Spirit of Christ'.[11] The title of Christ as a 'Steersman' or 'Navigator' (*gûbernetâ* in Syriac) is also found in the Syriac, *Manichean Psalms*,[12] but the expression,

5. M. Himmelfarb, *Ascent to Heaven in Jewish and Christian Apocalypses*, 61.
6. *Ibidem*, 65.
7. A. Golitzin, "Temple and Throne of the Divine Glory; 'Pseudo-Macarius' and Purity of Heart, Together with Some Remarks on the Limitations and Usefulness of Scholarship", in H.A. Luckman & L. Kulzer (eds.), *Purity of Heart in Early Ascetic and Monastic Literature* (Minnesota, The Liturgical Press, 1999), 116-129.
8. See, II. 1.1-3, Maloney, 37-41.
9. II. 44.8, Maloney, 225.
10. II. 44.5, Maloney, 224.
11. II. 44.6, Maloney, 225. For Christ the Navigator, see II. 28.2.
12. *Manichaen Psalms*, Allberry, 136. See *Table III*, in 'Titles of Christ', Robert Murray, *Symbols of the Kingdom*, 362.

'winged Spirit of Christ' is very unusual. It appears to be a reference to the Gospel account of Christ's words of lament over Jerusalem.

> 'O Jerusalem, Jerusalem, killing the prophets and stoning those who are sent to you! How often would I have gathered your children together as a hen gathers her brood under her wings, and you would not!'
>
> *Matthew* 23:37[13]

In Collection I of the Macarian Homilies, there is an extended analogy of this dominical saying which metaphorically describes Christ, the 'Word' as a mother bird, and his Spirit as the protective wings of his commandments. The emphasis upon the bird's wings brooding the chicks by warming them to quicken them into (re)birth and flight, echoes the brooding, flapping, hovering exegesis of the Syriac Genesis and baptismal tradition.

> 'Oh inexpressible love and mercy and compassion of the Lord! He makes himself like a bird, in order that the errant soul may take refuge under his wings, and he speaks the life-giving Word. See, he unfolds his wings and receives the soul when it enters to find rest there.
> For as a ritually unclean bird it is reborn, firstly with a downy covering. It is then taken again under his wings, and in its first covering thoroughly heated by the warmth, and when its covering is removed it stays within its mothers' wings until it reaches the "measure of maturity" (*Ephesians* 4:13) of its mother so that it flies to heaven and is above all the hostile forces that want to tear it apart and destroy it.
>
> For the Lord says, "he who loves me will be loved by my Father and I will love him and reveal myself to him" (*John* 14:21b). And most of all the command is that we should enter into the wings of our mother. For the soul warmed by the Word, is strengthened to remove the covering and be reborn in the Spirit, and Christ, revealed to the soul, flows out with a, "boundless spring of water" (*John* 7:37-9), and a recreated mind. Know this, oh soul, if you are in the wings of your mother, do not leave.
> Oh the unfolded wings, oh the compassion of the Father. Amen.'[14]

B. The Wings of the Spirit Offer Divine Aid in the Fulfilling of the Commandments

The Macarian emphasis on the hard work (πόνος) and suffering (κόρος) required to obey the commandments of Christ, is tempered by teaching on the divine aid of the Holy Spirit. In the analogy above, drawn from the image of Christ as a mother hen with her chicks, the 'wings of our mother'

13. Revised Standard Version (1952). This dominical saying belongs to the Q sayings source. See Luke 13: 34-35 for the same quotation.
14. I.3.6.1-4., ed. Berthold, vol.1, 40-41, English trans., J. Court.

are promised to warm and protect the newly hatched soul until its 'downy plumage' moults and it grows to reach, 'the measure of the maturity of its mother' and can 'fly to heaven'.[15] These protective wings are specifically identified with Christ's commandments to love which transcend the obligations of the Jewish Law.[16] The homily ends with an exhortation and a warning: 'Know this, oh soul, if you are in the wings of your mother do not leave it, lest you be destroyed by serpents. For the Saviour came to renew and give life to the soul and to exhaust the enemy.'[17]

In a different homily[18], the question is raised, how can the Christian, 'reach with certainty and without risk, the blessed and divine way of righteousness, great understanding, and spiritual insight' with the necessary endurance and faith required by Scripture (2 Peter 2:21)? An analogy is then drawn with a steep and rugged mountain footpath, impassable for 'four-legged animals'. The homily continues:

> 'In the same way, the sublime commandments of the Gospel and the way of God is narrow and restrictive for worldly people who do not participate (μετέχω) in the Spirit of God.[19] Christians however, are rendered lightweight by the wings of the Holy Spirit. The commandments of Jesus are not heavy (Matt. 11:30) when, by the grace of the wings of the Holy Spirit, they travel through with great lightness and joy, the way which is narrow for other people. The teaching concludes: Yes, without the holy wings of the Spirit it is impossible to pursue the way- that is to say, to fulfil all the commandments of the Lord with purity, perfection and without reproach — and thus to be judged worthy to reach the gateway to the kingdom of heaven.' [20]

Hermann Dörries has observed that one of the significant differences in the understanding of the activity of the Holy Spirit between Basil and Macarius is with respect to the commandments.[21] Whereas Basil emphasised the Christian's moral worthiness as a prerequisite for reception of the Holy Spirit (even at baptism),[22] Macarius focused upon the moral empowerment of divine grace. In Plested' s view, this was because of his, 'acute sense of the power of indwelling sin' and the need for 'liberation from the inhering passions.'[23] In the passages here cited, the Macarian

15. I. 3.6.1-4., ed. Berthold, vol.1, 40-41, English trans., J. Court.
16. I. 3.6.3.
17. I.3.6.4.
18. III. 16.1.1-1.3, ed. Desprez, 179-182. My translation.
19. III. 16.1.2.
20. III. 16.1.3.
21. H. Dörries, *Die Theologie des Makarios-Symeon* (Göttingen, 1978), 440.
22. Basil the Great, *Shorter Rules* 204 (1217B): "If we do not accomplish all the commandments of the Lord [...] we cannot expect to be held worthy of the Holy Spirit."
23. M. Plested, *The Macarian Legacy*, 50, fn 21.

'wings of the Spirit' seem to function both as the essential spirit of the Gospel commandments and as the means to put them into practice through the effective power of the Holy Spirit. Desprez observes that it is not always clear if this kind of teaching refers to mystical experience or an interior purification of spiritual vices.[24] For example, in III. 25.6.1., 'the good works of righteousness' are joined to the 'secret thoughts of the heart purified by the Spirit'. Here, as in Gregory of Nyssa' s, *Life of Moses*, asceticism and mysticism are inextricably bound together.[25]

From the lack of parallel examples, it would seem that the Macarian usage of the metaphor of the 'wings of the Spirit' for the teaching and practice of the Gospel commandments was an innovation. While there are no literary parallels in the early Syriac tradition, it does reflect the basic balance between righteousness and grace in this ascetic ethos where the 'stripping' (*msarrqûtā*) of the self to literally imitate Christ's life was believed to be aided at every step by the 'Power'. In the *Book of Steps*, where the 'perfect' were expected to perform a second 'hidden stripping of the heart',[26] by renouncing family and possessions and voluntarily choose celibacy, itinerancy and the way of the Cross, there is a recognition that because 'remnants of sin' still lodge in the heart, this path is too difficult without the aid of the 'pledge of the Spirit'.[27]

C. The Christian Escapes Enemies and Ascends into the Divine Milieu on the 'Wings of the Spirit'

In Homily III. 4.2.1-2, the birds who, aided by the air currents, 'ascend lightly into the air with the aid of their wings', are contrasted with earthbound animals. This analogy is used to highlight the distinction between the 'spiritual intelligence' (νοῦς πνευματικός) and the 'fleshly intelligence' (νοῦς σαρκικός).

> 'It is the same for the intelligence which has been purified and has acquired spiritual wings, every flight it ascends into the heavens, drawn into the air of divinity (τὸν ἀέρα τῆς θεότητος). But the bestial intelligence, savage and materialistic, wallows on the ground, crawling and searching the desert places.'[28].

24. V. Desprez, *Pseudo-Macaire*, 62.

25. This interpretation by Anthony Meredith of Gregory's 'ethico-mystical programme' in his *Gregory of Nyssa*, The Early Church Fathers Series (London, Routledge, 1999), 100, will be discussed in my Part 3.

26. *Liber Graduum* 12.1, English trans, Robert Murray, *Symbols*, 264.

27. Mêmre 3.11 (*P.S* 68: 18-69:4), English trans, R. A. Kitchen & M.F.G. Parmentier, *The Book of Steps*, 32.

28. III.4.2.2, ed. Desprez, 99.

In a similar fashion, in the 'Parable of the Mother-bird and her Fledglings', the air is seen as the natural environment for 'the children of God', who have outgrown vice and 'fortified by the Spirit and having the skies for their abode, no longer fear the ferocity of unclean spirits'.[29]

These analogies may be compared with a passage by Origen,[30] and in very similar fashion, Gregory of Nyssa, who described the Christian's moral and contemplative life as an ascent on eagle's wings above the sticky spiders-web of 'luxuries, honours, popular repute and various desires', spun by beasts below.[31] Desprez[32] suggests that the wings language in the Macarian similes was borrowed from the Alexandrian School and shared the influence of popular Platonic imagery from the, *Phaedrus*. Here, Socrates described the life of the philosopher who by rational detachment from the material world and contemplation of the eternal Forms could regrow the immortal wings he once possessed in pre-existence.[33] In the opinion of Deprez, Macarian flight imagery symbolises, 'l'agilité de la contemplation'[34] and 'l'absence de soucis'.[35] There is however a distinctive Macarian emphasis upon dependence upon divine grace which mitigates against any sense that wings could be grown by purely moral or intellectual effort (Origen speaks of Christians 'fashioning wings for themselves'). Further, the Macarian sense of the radical nature of sin in the heart, which he described as a 'demonic infestation' clearly could not be exorcised by noetic contemplation alone.

> 'To fly into the divine air and enjoy the liberty of the Holy Spirit (2 Corinthians 3:18) may be one's desire, but if he does not have wings given to him, he cannot. Let us pray to God to give us "the wings of a dove" (Psalm 55:7) of the Holy Spirit so that we may fly to Him and find rest and that He may separate and take away from our soul and body such an evil wind, namely, sin itself, inhabiting the members of our soul and body. For this He alone is able to do.'[36]

An interesting aspect to these three passages cited above, is the association of bird and wing imagery with 'the divine air', which is a frequent metaphor in the *Homilies*.[37] In the Syriac eschatological tradition, where

29. III. 16.2.5. ed. Deprez, 186.
30. Origen, *An Exhortation to Martyrdom*, 15, English trans, R.A.Greer (New York, Paulist Press, 1979), p. 52.
31. Gregory of Nyssa, *Treatise on the Inscriptions of the Psalms*, 8: 52, E. trans., R.E.Heine, (Oxford Early Christian Studies (Oxford, OUP Press, 1995), 108-9.
32. V. Desprez, *Pseudo-Macaire*, 180, fn1.
33. Plato, *Phaedrus* 245c-249d.
34. See for example, II.1.9.2 & II.2.3.
35. See I.14.22 & II. 30.6.
36. II. 2.6. Maloney, 45.
37. 'The divine air' is mentioned in I. 4.30.5.8: II.2.2; II.11 12; & II. 49.3. See also, the 'air of divinity', II. 47.2: III 4.2.2.

'flying' to heaven or in heaven is a common image, breezes or wind are associated with the divine milieu because they share the same noun as spirit/Spirit. For example, in Ephrem' s, *Hymns of Paradise,* the spiritual breezes 'suckle spiritual beings'.[38] Brock comments 'Just as air is essential for all life here, so too in Paradise is it the spiritual counterpart of air which sustains all transfigured existence there'.[39] In the light of this symbolism, it may be asked whether the *Macarian* image of the bird flying in the divine air is a way of representing the absolute dependence of the Christian upon the vivifying and energising Presence of the Spirit, which Macarius calls, the 'life of the soul' (ζωοποίησις ψυχῆς).

This observation opens the possibility of a second line of interpretation. Perhaps the Macarian term, 'spiritual intelligence' should be understood in terms of the Syriac anthropological category of the 'intellectual spirit' (*tar'itha*). In the eschatological teaching of both Aphrahat and Ephrem, the intellectual spirit which has been reborn through baptism and sanctified by the indwelling Spirit of Holiness, will be reunited with a glorified body and soul at the resurrection. In Paradise, it will fly to join Christ the Bridegroom, and be united with Him in the heavenly 'bridal chamber' (*gnônâ*).[40] In similar vein, Macarius described the joy of the day of resurrection when 'by the power of the Sun of Righteousness, the glory of the Holy Spirit rises up from within, covering and warming the bodies of the saints'. He compared it to the first month of Spring 'Xanthicus' in the Persian calendar.[41]

There are instances in Macarian teaching however, when this promised resurrection experience is anticipated in the present life of the 'perfect'. In the only reference to the primordial Adamic wings, there is an important insight into this view.

> 'When God created Adam, He did not furnish him with material wings as birds have, but prepared for him the wings of the Holy Spirit. The same He plans on giving him at the resurrection, to lift him and direct him wherever the Spirit wishes. These wings the saints already now are deemed to possess to fly up mentally to the realm of heavenly thoughts.'[42]

In this teaching, which is repeated in all three major collections, the future hopes for a transfigured body-soul-spirit are considered to have been realised on earth among the 'saints'. In this light, Macarian ascent language may be interpreted in terms of a radically realised eschatology which shares the

38. *H.Parad.* 9:9, English trans, S. Brock, *Hymns on Paradise*, 139.
39. Ibid.,135.
40. For a discussion of Syriac bridegroom and Bridal Chamber imagery see, S. Brock, *The Luminous Eye*, 115-30.
41. II.5.8, Maloney, 73.
42. I. 48.6.9 // II.5.11 // III 12b.

apocalyptic motif of the ascent of the sage to heaven. It would seem that Macarian teaching implied that it is possible through the agency of the 'wings of the Spirit', working in the spiritual intelligence, to fly through the divine air to the heavenly Jerusalem. For the 'saint' who serves the visible church and the 'hidden church' of the heart on earth there can be a simultaneous translation by grace into the divine milieu of 'the heavenly bridal chamber of the kingdom' and 'eternal salvation'.[43]

D. The 'Wings of the Spirit' Facilitate Prayer and Contemplation

There is a sense in which every Macarian usage of the metaphor of the 'wings of the Spirit' is related to the presence and empowering agency of the Holy Spirit. However, in a reflection of the rich Syriac tradition which associated the wings with states of prayer, religious exaltation and enlightenment, in the *Macarian Homilies*, there are examples which highlight direct personal experience of the Holy Spirit. Stewart observes that while for Origen, the spiritual senses were a 'faculty of intellectual and spiritual perception', for Macarius αἴσθησις also involved 'actual perception or experience'.[44] For example, grace as a mother is described leading the soul εἰς αἴσθησιν καὶ ἐπίγνωσιν of the heavenly Father'. [45] Stewart comments: 'here any distinction between "knowledge" and "experience", faculty and sensation disappears.'[46]

The image of light (φῶς) or illumination (φωτισμός) is used throughout the *Macriana* as a synonym for grace and the divine presence. It brings both enlightened perception, knowledge, and 'a far greater gift',[47] the real presence of the divine shining 'substantially' (ὑποστατικῶς) in the soul.[48] Golitzin has shown that Macarius often linked these descriptions of the *visio dei/gloriae* in the heart with a list of proof-texts from the Gospel of John and the Pauline Epistles as well as accounts of Ezekiel's vision, the Transfiguration on Mount Tabor, the descent of the Spirit on the Day of Pentecost and Saul's vision on the road to Damascus.[49] He claims that for Macarius, the heart/soul/intellect/inner man (terms which

43. II. 4. 7, Maloney, 53.
44. Columba Stewart, *Working the Earth of the Heart*, 124.
45. III. 27.4.30.
46. Columba Stewart, 127.
47. I.24.14; I.58.1.1.
48. I. 58.2.; I. 28.2.1.
49. A. Golitzen, *Temple and Throne of Divine Glory*, 121-22.

seem to be used almost interchangeably) has become the spiritual successor to Sinai or Zion: 'The heart is, potentially, the locus of theophany, and that potential is real.'[50] In these heightened spiritual states, the 'wings of the Spirit' seem to symbolize two aspects.

Firstly, the 'wings of the Spirit' purify the spiritual intellect in order to gather the distracted and multiple thoughts of the soul 'into one great divine thought'.[51] Plested has argued that this is an 'anagogic' element. Here, perfection is related to a process of 'intellection' (κατανόησις) as the *nous* rises out of materiality and ascends towards the divine. In his view such noetic passages 'served as a corrective to the crudely material understanding of spiritual experience characteristic of the Messalians.'[52] However, the Macarian term, *monotropos* (literally 'in one place') could refer to practices of recollection in prayer deriving from a Syriac tradition. This study has demonstrated that the aim of becoming 'single-minded' (*monotropos*) can be interpreted in a Syriac tradition. In the 4th century *Demonstrations* of Aphrahat it had become an essential element in the focused prayer-life of the consecrated, *îhîdāyâ* ('single (minded)-one') who took ascetic vows before being baptised under the wings of the hovering Spirit.

Gilles Quispel and Dom A. Baker have suggested that the Macarian teaching on focused prayer may be linked to the traditions of the early 2nd century *Gospel of Thomas*.[53] This collection of sayings (*logia*) attributed to Jesus, was probably written in Greek in Syrian Antioch but elements reflects an oral Aramaic Gospel sayings-source.[54] The secret sayings of Jesus to the Apostle, Judas Didymos Thomas, emphasise a discipleship of committed seeking and finding truth. For example:

> 'Jesus said, "Those who seek should not stop seeking until they find. When they find, they will be disturbed. When they are disturbed, they will marvel, and will rule over all."'
>
> *Gospel of Thomas* Saying 2

These Syriac single-minded aims and practices for 'turning the attention' Godwards (the literal meaning of 'repentance', in Greek, μετάνοια) are rooted in early Jewish-Christian traditions and challenge the view that

50. *Ibidem*, 123.
51. III. 18.2.2.
52. M. Plested, *The Macarian Legacy*, 65-6.
53. See A. Baker, "Pseudo- Macarius and the Gospel of Thomas", *Vigiliae Christianae* 18 (1964): 215-25, and Gilles Quispel, "The Syrian Thomas and the Syrian Macarius", *Vigiliae Christianae* 18 (1964), 226-35.
54. For a survey of the scholarly discussion of the dating and provenance of the Gospel of Thomas, see, Richard Valantasis, *The Gospel of Thomas*, New Testament Reading (Routledge, London, 1997), 12-21.

Macarius was thinking fundamentally in Greek philosophic terms. It appears more plausible, as Columba Stewart argues, that he creatively 'translated' Syriac spiritual teaching into a Greek conceptual framework for his audience.[55]

That the 'wings of the Spirit' were believed to facilitate holistic religious experiences rather than primarily metaphysical intellection can be inferred from other Macarian teaching. For example, from the 'Parable of the mother-bird and her fledglings'.

> 'The soul is "borne and guided" (βασταξόμενος καὶ ὁδηγούμενος) on the wings of the Spirit towards visions and revelations of the heavenly mysteries, towards those ineffable spiritual contemplations which the language of flesh cannot express.'[56]

Desprez notes that here, the usual Greek term for contemplation/direct spiritual perception (θεωρία), is used in the plural, suggesting actual physical visions.[57] In an homily devoted to teaching on prayer, Macarius also used very similar expressions before going on to speak personally of a vision of a cross of light 'which plunged itself deep in the inner man'.[58] He then described two spiritual states resulting from the initial vision, both the work of grace. Sometimes, 'it quiets all my parts and my heart so that the soul with the greatest joy seems to be a guileless child'. At such moments he felt deep joy and overwhelming dispassionate love (ἀπάθεια) for everyone irrespective of faith or race.[59] In the second spiritual state, Macarius had the sense of being, 'the son of a king', entering into doors in a long succession of 'mansions' where 'new and amazing wonders are disclosed to him'. This analogy, while undiscussed by Golitzin, seems to substantiate his thesis that Macarian spiritual teaching was influenced by the *hekhalot* rabbinic literature from the Babylonian Talmudic period (200 AD-600 AD).[60] In this form of apocalyptic Jewish mysticism sages ascended through a succession of heavenly *hekhalot* (temples or palaces) until they reached the highest heaven. Here, it was believed, surrounded by the heavenly court of angels, was situated the chariot-throne of God (*merkabah*), which Ezekiel saw on the banks of the Chebar. The sage having received revelations and secrets

55. Columba Stewart, *Working the Earth of the Heart*, 234-40.
56. III. 16.2.5, ed. Desprez, 185.
57. V. Desprez, *Pseudo-Macaire*, 185, fn 1.
58. II. 8.3 & 6. Maloney, 81 & 83.
59. II.8.6., Maloney, 83.
60. See A. Golitzin, "Recovering the 'Glory of Adam'", 288ff. & 305-7 and "Temple and Throne of the Divine Glory", 118-22.

of the celestial realm then descended to earth.[61] Golitzin observes that in the Christian appropriation of Aphrahat and Macarius, this visionary experience seems to have been considered as a descent into the heart/soul in imitation of the humble self-emptying of Christ.[62]

61. See G. Scholem, *Major Trends in Jewish Mysticism*, 3rd revised edition (Jerusalem, Schocken Pub. House, 1973), 40-79.
62. A. Golitzin, "Recovering the 'Glory of Adam'", 300-01.

CHAPTER 7

GLORIFICATION OF THE SOUL AS THE CHARIOT-THRONE OF GOD

The awesome Macarian 'allegorical interpretation' of the prophet Ezekiel's vision by the River Chebar in Babylon, is a fitting place to end this part of my study.[1] This extended interpretation is the opening homily in the second collection of the *Macriana* and introduces the theme of glorification, the transfiguration of the believer through the possession of the Holy Spirit. It begins with a summary of the account in the Hebrew Bible of the appearance of God enthroned above the winged Cherubim in a chariot. The verses from Chapter 1 of the biblical, *Book of Ezekiel*, read:

> 'As I looked, behold, a stormy wind came out of the north, and a great cloud, with brightness round about it, and fire flashing forth continually, and in the midst of the fire, as it were gleaming bronze. and from the midst of it came the likeness of four living creatures. And this was their appearance, they had the form of men, but each had four faces, and each of them four wings .... Under their wings on their four sides they had human hands and the four had their faces and their wings thus: their wings touched one another .... And each went straight forward, without turning as they went, wherever the spirit would go, they went, without turning as they went.'
>
> *Ezekiel* 1:4-6, 8-9, 12.[2]

Macarius began his interpretation by commenting that the vision, which the prophet saw 'in ecstasy or in a trance', was 'only signifying and foreshadowing something no less hidden, something divine and mysterious' that 'has only been revealed in our time, the end of ages, when Christ appeared'.[3] For Macarius, steeped in the Syrian Christian Antiochene method of biblical interpretation, important Old Testament symbols acted as divine hints or 'types' of the coming of the new dispensation in Christ. The chariot-throne of God which Ezekiel saw prefigured the transformation of fallen humanity through the incarnation and passion of Christ: 'For the prophet was viewing the mystery of the human soul that would receive its Lord and would become his throne of glory.'

1. II.1.1-3., Maloney, 37-39.
2. English, *Revised Standard Version* (London, Oxford Univ. Press, 1971) 883.
3. II.1.2, Maloney p. 37.

In the following lines, Macarius described this transformation as a transfiguration into light and glory. As in Ezekiel's vision, the living creatures moved within wheels covered with eyes, so it is with the sanctified Christian.

> 'The soul that is deemed to be judged worthy to participate in the light of the Holy Spirit by becoming its throne and habitation, and is covered with the beauty of ineffable glory of the Spirit, becomes all light, all face, all eye. There is no part of the soul that is not full of the spiritual eyes of light.'[4]

This remarkable teaching on the mysticism of light was probably influenced by Ephrem's commentary on the vision of Ezekiel, whom he claimed, had a 'luminous eye' (*'ayna shaphita*).[5] The lucidity of spiritual perception acts as an inner-eye of vision beyond discursive thought.

The Macarian description of the chariot-throne is followed by an allegorical interpretation of the four living creatures as the four faculties of the soul: will, conscience, the mind and power of loving. These are ruling characteristics for moral believers, 'dominant powers that are superior to others' ... 'it is through such that the chariot of the soul is directed and it is in these that God resides.'[6] This offers the clearest example of a definite influence of the Platonic myth of the charioteer of the soul from the *Phaedrus*.[7] Socrates described two reins which controlled the winged horses that lead the soul on its heavenly ascent or earthly descent. He named them: the *logistikon* (the rule of reason) and the *epithymetikon* (rule of appetite and desire). While Macarius would have known this popular teaching in the Greek-speaking environment of Roman Syria, he clearly reworked it in a radically reinterpreted form. The four 'faculties' (literally, 'thoughts', *logismoi*) of the soul however, now become the four 'living creatures' (Ezekiel's, *hayyot*) whose wings bear and move the chariot-throne of God. In contrast to Plato's charioteer, the philosopher's, *logistikon*, it is Christ who is the 'Rider'.

> 'The Rider, then, is carried by the chariot and the animals with all eyes, or, in a way, he is carried by every soul that has become his throne and exists now as eye and light. He is mounted on the soul and guides it with the reins of the Spirit, directing it according to his knowledge of the way.'[8]

4. II.1.2, Ibid.
5. Ephrem, *Hymns of the Church* 11:4, cited by S. Brock, *The Luminous Eye: The Spiritual World Vision of Saint Ephrem the Syrian* (Cistercian Study Series 124, Kalamazoo, 1992), p. 73.
6. II.1.3, Maloney p. 38.
7. Plato, *Phaedrus*, 248b (see also 249d-257b).
8. *Macarian Homilies* II.1.3, Maloney p. 38.

Golitzin comments: 'This is no surrender of the Gospel to the Hellenes, but the buckling into harness, like Plato's *logistikon*, of the great Greeks in the service of the Gospel beatitude: the pure in heart shall see God.'[9]

In his study of Syriac temple and throne imagery, Golitzin has not commented upon the 'wings of the Spirit', but from this study it is perhaps possible to add another aspect to his discussion of Macarian teaching. For it was by an innovative use of this rich metaphor, steeped in Syriac Christian tradition, that Macarius expressed his conviction that it was through the loving guidance, inspiration and dynamic power of the Holy Spirit that the soul is finally led to the theophany of the indwelling throne and into what Macarius innovatively and radically named 'mystical communion' (μυστική κοινωνία) with God.[10]

> 'Holy souls are led and guided by the Spirit of Christ, who directs them where he wishes them to go. Sometimes he leads them by his will through heavenly thoughts, sometimes through the body. Wherever he wishes, there they minister to him. Just as the feet of birds are the wings, so the heavenly light of the Spirit takes up the wings of thoughts worthy of the soul and leads and directs the soul as it knows best.'[11]

9. A. Golitzin, 'Temple and Throne', p. 129.
10. Macarius introduced the term, 'mystical communion/participation' (*mystiké koinōnia*) into the Christian vocabulary, see II. 4.15.2; II.10.2 & II 47.17. See *Epistola Magna* for term 'mystical union' (*mystiké synousia*), E. trans, G.A. Maloney, 'The Great Letter', in, *Pseudo-Macarius*, p. 257.
11. II.1.9., Maloney, p. 42.

PART III

A MACARIAN SYNTHESIS OF SYRIAC AND GREEK WINGS METAPHORS?

CHAPTER 8

THE HOLY SPIRIT AND THE NICENE CREED

In 325 AD, the Christian bishops were summoned by imperial edict to the first Ecumenical Council. The Roman Empire under Constantine was moving to embrace Christianity as the state religion, but who defined this new faith? The aim at Nicaea was to find a credal consensus which united the Church in the face of the Arian rejection of the full divinity of Christ. The final creed confessed the belief in Jesus Christ:

> 'God from God, Light from Light, true God from true God, Begotten not made, Consubstantial (*homoousios*) with the Father.'

The Holy Spirit was included almost as an afterthought:

> 'We believe in the Holy Spirit.'

The dogma and definition of *homoousios*, far from uniting the Church, provoked factionalism and schism depending upon the interpretation and personal opinions of local bishops and the current emperor. The Cappadocian Fathers, in seeking to champion the Nicene Creed and develop its trinitarian implications, represented only a small minority of orthodox congregations struggling to survive. Basil graphically described the doctrinal conflicts as a pitched naval battle.

> 'Imagine, if you will, the rival fleets driven into confusion by a raging tempest, while thick darkness falls from the clouds and blackens the entire scene, so that signals cannot be recognised, and one can no longer distinguish between friend and foe .... All four winds meet together and dash one fleet against the other. Meanwhile some of the combatants are betraying each other, some are deserting in the middle of the battle; while others at the same time are compelled, whilst the wind drives them on, to urge their boats forward against the enemy.'[1]

Emerging from this context of doctrinal controversy and personality conflicts, the Cappadocian Fathers crafted their theological writings which focused upon their evolving perception of One God as a Trinity of Persons. The extent to which the influence of teaching on the Holy Spirit from Syriac Christianity, and in particular through the writings of the

1. Basil the Great, *On the Holy Spirit*, Eng. trans. David Anderson, (Popular Patristic Series, New York SVS Press, 1980), p. 114.

Macriana played a part in this process will be explored in this part. That there was interaction is clear, both Basil and Gregory of Nyssa refer to spiritual teachers from the Orient whom they have met or read. The precise nature of literary and theological dependency however, is an on-going complex scholarly debate.

The crowning culmination of the Cappadocian' s theological work, was the addition of a new clause on the Holy Spirit to the Nicene Creed at the synod of one hundred and fifty bishops at Constantinople in 381 AD. Gregory of Nyssa played a leading role in this Ecumenical Council, his brother, Basil having died prematurely two years before. In this revised confession, the Holy Spirit is affirmed as fully divine, as both the agent of sanctification and inspired biblical prophesy and the source of all created existence.

> 'We believe in the Holy Spirit, the Lord, the Giver of Life,
> who proceeds from the Father:
> who with the Father and the Son together is worshipped and glorified.
> Who has spoken through the prophets.'

CHAPTER 9

'WINGS LANGUAGE': THE SCHOLARLY DEBATE ON MACARIAN DEPENDENCY

In this study so far, I have explored the Macarian metaphor of the 'wings of the Spirit' from an early Syriac Christian angle of perspective. My presupposition has been that while the teachings of the *Macarian Homilies* were produced by a Greek-speaking monastic elder, they represent a Syriac indigenous tradition interacting with the wider Greek Christian ethos. While this interpretation is accepted in general to a lesser or greater extent by modern scholars, the use of 'wings language' is still assumed to be part of a cluster of 'mystical' and 'Platonic' themes borrowed by Macarius from Gregory of Nyssa's later writings. In the opinion of, Vincent Desprez, these themes include the tension between a doctrine of the spiritual senses and the incomprehensibility of God, the dignity of the soul created in the image of God, the role of the intellectual mind (νοῦς) in the spiritual life, the use of spiritual exegesis closely allied to the allegorical method of Origen, and the ascension of the soul towards the Good and Beautiful on the wings of the soul.[1] The consensus in current scholarship is summed up by Werner Jaeger, first general editor of the *Gregorii Nysseni Opera*: 'Macarius embraces with all his heart and ardent fervour the mystical and ascetical theology begun with the speculation of Origen and formulated most clearly in the works of Gregory of Nyssa.' [2]

In 1954, Jaeger initiated an unprecedented new wave of research into *Macriana*, when he produced a new critical edition of Gregory's last ascetical treatise, *De Instituto Christiano* and claimed that it was the source for the Macarian 'Great Letter' or *Epistola Magna* which is *Logos* 1 in the Macarian Collection I. Jaeger argued that 'Macarius is paraphrasing a text of Gregory of Nyssa from beginning to end.'[3]

1. V. Desprez, *Pseudo-Macaire*, p. 53-55.
2. W. Jaeger, *Two Rediscovered Works of Ancient Christian Literature: Gregory of Nyssa and Macarius* (Leiden, Brill, 1954), p. 229.
3. Ibid., p. 209.

The 'Great Letter' has two parts. The first (409C-420B) deals with carnal-minded and self-centred passions (παθή) which prevent the heart from purifying its desires and becoming an abode of the indwelling Holy Spirit. It offers advice on how to reach a state of inner peace and personal integration (ἀπάθεια). The second part of the letter (420C-441) addresses loose-knit monastic communities and their elders, offering advice on communal spirituality. The emphasis is upon attaining humility and purity of heart and practicing mindful continuous prayer. The style of the treatise is typically Macarian with simple examples and anecdotes drawn from a rural context, peppered with biblical citations, and his usual themes and teaching on, 'the adorable and Holy Spirit'. The following analogy, drawn from viniculture is typical.

> 'When we cultivate a vineyard, the whole of our attention and labour is given in the expectation of the harvest. If there is no vintage, all our work is in vain. Similarly, if through the activity of the Spirit we do not perceive within ourselves the fruits of love, peace and the other qualities mentioned by St. Paul (Galatians 5:22), then our labour for the sake of virginity, prayer, psalmody, fasting and vigil is useless.'[4]

The claim of Jaeger for Gregorian precedence for the 'Great Letter' has been challenged. First by J. Gribomont who showed that the vocabulary, biblical exegesis and theology of *De Instituto* belonged to the Macarian model.[5] In 1984, Reinhold Staats published a parallel version of both treatises in order to demonstrate that Gregory reworked two-thirds of an original letter by 'Symeon of Mesopotamia'. The inelegancies of the rustic and personal style of the *Great Letter* were seen to have been ironed out to present in a more cultured and philosophical style all the essentials of the original teaching.[6] In the opinion of Staat' s, Gregory had attempted to translate Macarian ideas on the ascetical life into a literary language acceptable to the Greek intelligentsia. This is an important observation when I examine the sources and theology of Gregory's 'wings language' at the conclusion of this study.

4. Macarius, *The Great Letter*, Eng. trans. George Maloney (Classics of Western Spirituality, New York, Paulist Press, 1992), p. 268.

5. J. Gribomont, 'Le De instituto christiano et le Messalianisme de Grégoire de Nysse' *Studia Patristica* 5 (Berlin, 1962), pp. 312-22.

6. R. Staats (ed.), *Makarios-Symeon: Epistola Magna. Eine messalianische Mönchsregel und ihre Umschrift in Gregors von Nyssa, 'De Instituto Christiano'* (Göttingen, 1984).

CHAPTER 10

SYRO-MESOPOTAMIAN INFLUENCES ON THE CAPPADOCIAN FATHERS

The anteriority of the 'Great Letter' and the proof of Gregory's literary borrowing from a Macarian writing, shed new light upon the question of influence. Jaeger's assumption that Macarius was dependent upon the writings of the Cappadocian Fathers may prove to be over-simplistic. In Marcus Plested' s view, their relationship was one of mutual influence across cultural boundaries prompted by a shared concern for 'monastic reform and Trinitarian theology'.[1]

It is certainly possible that the Macarian homely, practical and pneumatic homilies, which insisted upon the sanctifying and perfecting power of the Holy Spirit, would have been welcomed as sound and inspiring by Basil and Gregory who were championing their polemic in defence of the divinity of the Holy Spirit in the face of neo-Arian imperial opposition. Caught between the radical faction of Basil's former mentor, Eustathius of Sebaste, who rejected the divinity of the Holy Spirit (the self-proclaimed 'Spiritfighters' or *Pneumatomachoi*) and on-going Christological arguments with the neo-Arian theologian, Eunomius, they must have welcomed teachings reflecting a charismatic vision for Christian community life. Basil, saw himself as a monastic reformer and wrote his own 'Shorter' and 'Longer Rules' (*Asceticon*). The Macarian emphasis upon Spirit-filled fraternities chimed with his aspirations for 'brotherhoods' (ἀδελφότης), modelled upon the first church in Jerusalem.[2]

In Basil's book, 'On the Holy Spirit' (*Liber de Spiritu Sancto*), there is evidence that his pneumatology was influenced by traditions from Syriac churches. The treatise systematically discussed all the witnesses available in Scripture and in the baptismal and liturgical traditions which referred to the Holy Spirit. In a lengthy grammatical discussion, he defended the usage of the Trinitarian formula in the Doxology of the non-Greek-speaking

1. M. Plested, *The Macarian Legacy*, p. 57.

2. For the thesis that Basil aimed to model both his *cenobia* and the local churches upon the 'apostolic life' and *koinōnia* in material possessions and spiritual gifts, see Paul J. Fedwick, *The Church and the Charismata of Leadership in Basil of Caesarea* (Toronto, Pontifical Institute of Mediaeval Studies, 1979).

churches of the East (and which he had adopted controversially in his diocese): 'Glory to the Father with (μετὰ) the Son together (σύν) with the Holy Spirit.' Discussing its contemporary use in the Eastern liturgy he remarked:

> 'I once heard a certain Mesopotamian, a man experienced in both language and accurate knowledge, say that in his country it is not possible to say the doxology in any other way, since the grammatical rules of their language force them to use their equivalent of the conjunction, "and". Our Cappadocian dialect is similar; perhaps the Spirit foresaw how useful this word would be, when it gave the gift of tongues to the disciples!'[3]

In his last book, a commentary on Genesis (*Homiliae in Hexaemeron*), Basil again referred to the opinion of 'a certain Syrian' whom he regarded to be both highly authoritative and worthy of wider dissemination on exegetical and liturgical matters.[4] Brock suggests that these references led the Church historian, Sozomen, to assume that Basil greatly admired the erudition of Ephrem,[5] an observation which later led to ever more elaborate hagiographical accounts of a meeting between the two theologians.[6] The recent scholarly debate has concluded that the influential Syrian was either Basil's acquaintance, Diodore of Tarsus,[7] or more likely, Diodore' s teacher (and founder of the 'Antiochene School') Eusebius of Emesa.[8]

What is of interest for this discussion, is the evidence that Basil knew from a scholion of this unnamed teacher, that the Greek *Septuagint* translation of the 'wind/spirit of God moving' over the waters of creation in Genesis 1:2b (πνεῦμα θεοῦ ἐπεφέρετο), lacked the nuances of the Hebrew metaphorical meanings connected with the Spirit of God 'who broods like a bird over its young'.[9] This exegetical observation in Basil's, *Homilies on the Hexaemeron* 2.6, was later cited by others or intermediaries, for example Jerome[10], Ambrose and Augustine. Thus it was through one of the last writings of Basil that the Syriac tradition of the Holy Spirit

3. Basil the Great, *Liber Spiritu Sancto* 29.74, Anderson, p. 111.
4. Basil the Great, *Homiliae in Hexaemeron* 2.6.
5. Sozomen's, *Ecclesiastical History* III.16, E. trans., C.D. Hartranft in, 'A Select Library of Nicene and Post-Nicene Fathers', Series II, vol.2 (Oxford, 1891), cited by S. Brock in, *St Ephrem the Syrian : Hymns on Paradise*, pp. 15-19.
6. For a discussion on the hypothetical episode, see O. Rousseau, 'Le rencontre de S. Ephrem et de S. Basile', *L'Orient Syrien* 2 (1957), pp. 261-84.
7. J. Pouchet, 'Les rapports de Basile de Césarée avec Diodore de Tarse', *BLE* 87 (1986), pp. 243-72.
8. L. Van Rompay, 'L'informateur Syrien de Basile de Césarée. A propos de Genèse 1,2,' *Orientalia Christiana Periodica* 58 (1992), pp. 245-51. For my discussion of the exegesis of Eusebius of Emesa on Genesis 1 v.2b see, p. 10 and fn. 19.
9. Basil the Great, *Homiliae in Hexaemeron* 2.6, ed. Giet (*SC* 26), pp. 166-171.
10. Jerome, *Quaestiones Hebraicae* ad. loc., ed. Antin-Lagarde, p. 3.

as a mother bird hovering over the waters of creation entered into the Christian traditions of the late Roman Empire!

The importance of this shift in Western exegesis cannot be underestimated. In his book, 'On the Holy Spirit', Basil had restricted his theological reflections to 'proof texts' from the Scriptures and examples from the apostolic tradition of the churches. Trained in logic and dialectics in the Athenian Academies, he always worked from the inductive method. Without a biblical or liturgical reference he could not assert the full divinity of the Holy Spirit, so in his book Basil avoided general statements concerning the Spirit such as "God the Holy Spirit" but rather concluded on the evidence that 'the Holy Spirit partakes of the fullness of divinity.'[11] The discovery of the original meaning of Genesis 1:2b opened the possibility to consider the Holy Spirit as the divine agent of created existence.

Basil ended his exegesis on the 'brooding' Spirit in Genesis with the conclusion that 'it is quite clear that the Holy Spirit is not without a share in the creative activity of God.' In a study of the pneumatology of the Cappadocian Fathers, Anthony Meredith argues that Basil's commentary here is of fundamental importance and without parallel because it is the only clear example where Basil accepted the creative function of the Holy Spirit.[12] In Meredith's view, the main reason that Basil did not apportion consubstantiality to the Spirit, even in his treatise, *On the Holy Spirit*, was because he could not 'emancipate himself from the Origenist tradition in which he worked' which restricted the action of the Holy Spirit to the sanctification of rational beings.[13]

In Gregory's, *On the Holy Spirit, Against the Macedonians, the Spirit Fighters*, [14] there is an obvious shift from this Origenist pneumatology. In Meredith's opinion, it was the fact that Gregory saw creation as 'the characteristic activity of God' and that he insisted upon the fully creative activity of the Spirit (as co-creative with the Father and the Son) which enabled him to vindicate the Spirit's title to full divinity.[15] According to Meredith, Gregory owed this 'substantial divergence from his brother' to

11. Basil the Great, *Liber Spiritu Sacto* 46.

12. A. Meredith, 'The Pneumatology of the Cappadocian Fathers and the Creed of Constantinople', *Irish Theological Quarterly* 48 (1981), p. 200-201.

13. Ibid., pp. 201 & 203-4. See, *Liber de Spiritu Sancto* 16.38 & 40 where Basil restricts the work of the Spirit to the sanctification of the rational order of creation alone.

14. F. Mueller, ed., *GNO* 111.1; E. trans. of III.1.105.19-110.23 by A. Meredith, 'Against the Macedonians', in *Gregory of Nyssa* (Early Church Fathers Series, London, Routledge, 1999), pp. 39-46.

15. A. Meredith, 'The Pneumatology', p. 206-7

the arguments used by Athanasius against the Tropici in his four *Letters to Serapion*. From the perspective of this study on the Syriac background to the 'wings of the Spirit', it is interesting to note that Gregory also knew of this tradition, which apportioned creative activity to the Holy Spirit, through his brother's *Hexaemeron*. It can only be conjectured how Basil, who was clearly shifting his 'economical' position in the struggle against the *Pneumatomachoi*, would have developed his pneumatology if he had lived longer.

After Basil's premature death in 379 AD, Gregory of Nyssa became a leading champion of Trinitarian theology and enjoyed imperial patronage as a key proponent of the Ecumenical Council of Constantinople in 380-1. It was here that he gave a speech in praise of ascetic 'Mesopotamians' whom he credited with renewing the charismata of the early Church:[16]

> 'They have like Abraham left their country, their family and the world at large. They look to heaven; they cut themselves off, so to say, from human life; they are superior to the passions of nature [...]. They do not struggle with words, they do not study rhetoric; but they have such power over the spirits [...] that they expel demons not through syllogistic arts but through the power of faith.'[17]

Staats has suggested that this is a reference to ascetic circles associated with Macarius.[18] Plested agrees that it is 'very plausible'.[19] A strong reason for assuming that Gregory was becoming increasingly influenced by the charismatic tendency associated with the Macarian writings was his absence from the Synod of Side (ca. 390). This gathering of Greek bishops was summoned by Amphilochius of Iconium to counter the perceived threat of 'Messalianism'. This term is Syriac for 'praying ones', and was associated in the bishops' minds with a jumble of Eastern excesses including religious enthusiasm, radical asceticism and a rejection of work. Marcus Plested comments: 'None of our immediate sources are able to provide a convincing picture of its nature.' [20]

Whether Gregory was not invited to the synod because of his sympathies or simply absented himself to avoid controversy, it seems to have been the culmination of a marked change in his life. Withdrawing from public life,

16. Gregory of Nyssa, *In Gregorii ordinationem* (or *In suam ordinationem*), ed. Gebhardt, *GNO* 9.
17. E. trans., M. Plested, *The Macarian Legacy*, p. 54.
18. R. Staats, 'Die Asketen aus Mesopotamien in der Rede des Gregor von Nyssa, *In suam ordinationem*', *Vigiliae Christianae* 21 (1967), pp. 165-79.
19. M. Plested, *The Macarian Legacy*, p. 54.
20. Ibid., p. 19.

he devoted himself to the 'mystical' writings for which he is now best known. It was probably just before his death (ca. 395-6) that he composed his treatise based upon the Macarian *Great Letter*. Plested has pointed out that this writing gave an unusual emphasis, for Gregory, upon the 'primacy of prayer, the gift of the Holy Spirit and the theme of spiritual plenitude', suggesting 'his dependence upon the Macarian model'.[21]

The precise nature of the relationship between the later writings of Gregory and the Macarian corpus is highly complex and will require further research. Next, I shall make only a few general observations before discussing the comparative nature of their 'wings language'.

21. M. Plested, *The Macarian Legacy*, pp. 53-4.

CHAPTER 11

MACARIUS AND GREGORY OF NYSSA: A CROSS-FERTILISATION OF TRADITIONS AND TEACHING

Jaeger assumed Macarian dependency upon the basic structure of Gregory's 'neo-Platonic' programme for moral formation (μόρφωσις) leading to 'perfection' (τελείωσις) and 'participation' (μετανουσία) in God through imitation of the divine attributes. In his, *Early Christianity and Greek Paideia*, Jaeger argued that throughout Gregory's writings, the function of the Holy Spirit was to perfect this process of moral and intellectual growth through pedagogy of the 'worthy' soul.[1] Since the theme of spiritual and moral development, the growing of 'spiritual wings' (πτέρυγας πνευματικάς) and the pedagogy of the Spirit is a feature of some Macarian teaching, for example, the 'Parable of the Mother-bird and her Fledglings', Jaeger's thesis may be correct. On the other hand, however, the teaching on spiritual milk and meat and growth in stages of ascetic imitation of Christ towards perfection, is also a marked feature of the Syriac, *Book of Steps*. It seems possible that Macarius was influenced by both Cappadocian and Syriac teaching here. Gregory's stress upon virtue as an end in itself, however, is not shared in the *Macriana*. The teaching in the *Life of Moses*, that God is 'absolute virtue' (ἡ παντελὴς ἀρετή) and that 'whoever pursues true virtue participates in nothing other than God'[2] leaves no room for direct religious experience of the indwelling Holy Spirit or the divine light. As Norman Russell points out, Gregory's moral teaching implies that participation in God is 'only analogous' and exercised through the attributes/operations of virtue.[3]

Meredith describes the fundamental structure of Gregory's teaching as an 'ethico-mystical programme'.[4] In his opinion, there is a 'Platonic theorem' at the centre of Gregory's spiritual writings, which he describes

1. W. Jaeger, *Early Christianity and Greek Paideia* (Cambridge, Mass., 1961), pp. 86-99.
2. *Vita Moysis* 1.7, E. trans., A.J. Malherbe & E .Ferguson, *Gregory of Nyssa: The Life of Moses* (Classics of Western Spirituality, New York, Paulist Press, 1978), p. 31.
3. N. Russell, *The Doctrine of Deification in the Greek Patristic Tradition* (Oxford Early Christian Studies, Oxford Univ. Press, 2004) p. 232.
4. A. Meredith, *Gregory of Nyssa*, p. 8.

as 'the upward march of the created spirit to knowledge and enjoyment of God occasioned by the loveliness of God and demanding moral perfection as well as mental abstraction'. For Gregory, the 'driving' force is 'eros' (ἔρως), the unsatisfied desire to behold Beauty.[5] This emphasis upon the insatiable yearning to transcend both the senses and thoughts on an infinite quest to see God in the darkness (γνόφος) of pure faith and love is a central feature of both the *Life of Moses* and the *Commentary on the Song of Songs*. In contrast, these Gregorian themes of divine Beauty, the erotic desire for God, ἐπέκτασις and γνόφος are only rarely, if at all in evidence in Macarian spiritual teaching, suggesting they did not constitute the framework of his pneumatology.

In Plested's opinion, Gregory's emphasis upon divine darkness, which is in such contrast to the Macarian language of light and glory, 'does not constitute a fundamental distinction between their apophaticism'.[6] This may be the case on a philosophical level, but there is a sense of substance to the Macarian descriptions of divine light which is of a different symbolic order to Gregory's subtle descriptions of the mirror of the soul and the spiritual senses. For example, the awesome account of the vision of Ezekiel, while sharing some Platonic imagery, clearly belongs to a mysticism of light and transfiguration. The description of the soul transformed into the chariot throne of God, glowing with 'the ineffable glory of the Spirit' and becoming like the cherubic living creatures, 'all light, all face, all eye,' [7] could only have derived from a Jewish or Syriac background.

This discussion has so far highlighted some general similarities and differences between the mindset of the Cappadocian brothers, Basil and Gregory and the writer of the *Macarian Homilies*. I have shown that the discussion about intellectual or literary dependency is best approached within the context of their relationship of mutual admiration and influence. As we have seen, the Cappadocian Fathers, although working within a Christianised neo-Platonic and Philonic conceptual framework, were deeply appreciative of the Syriac tradition of asceticism and spiritual teaching rooted in a Jewish-Christian ethos. There is evidence of a cross-fertilisation of ideas and practices across the cultural boundaries. In the Greek *Macarian Homilies*, the blurring of the contours of Greek and Syriac religious metaphorical language may have been an intentional attempt to stretch inherited concepts and symbols in order to both bridge

5. Ibid., p. 85.
6. M. Plested, *The Macarian Legacy*, p. 56.
7. *Macarian Homilies* II.1.2, Maloney, p. 37.

the cultural divide and to express 'ineffable' religious experience. It is an open question with which I shall conclude, whether Gregory, towards the end of his life, also began to seek a religious language that forged a certain convergence between his growing mystical awareness of the transformative power of the Spirit of Christ and the Macarian metaphor of the 'wings of the Spirit'.

In this study I have explored the rich tradition of the metaphor of the 'wings of the Spirit' in Syriac Christianity from the 2nd to 4th centuries. Its usage in sacramental, devotional and proto-monastic literature demonstrates that it was a fundamental dimension of Syriac pneumatology linked to beliefs connected with the creative, sanctifying and enlightening power and presence of the Holy Spirit. I have demonstrated that it is possible to interpret the four main clusters of teaching on the 'wings of the Spirit' in the *Macarian Homilies* from within this cultural and religious tradition. Further, that in the Macarian usage, this teaching is closely linked to some other themes from the Syriac ascetic tradition; these include the nature and functions of the Spirit as a mother or mother bird, elements of realised eschatology linked with Jerusalem, the gracious mother, and the hidden church of the heart.

This calls for a reassessment of the perceived wisdom that Macarian wings language was simply an appropriation of Gregorian usage. For it follows logically, that if commentators such as Jaeger and Desprez are correct in arguing that the Macarian teaching on the 'wings of the Spirit' was simply borrowed from Gregory's 'neo-Platonic' usage of the 'wings of the soul', one would expect to find that metaphor embedded in teaching and clusters of themes similar to those in the *Macarian Homilies*. The evidence is negligible apart from some features in *Oratio* 15 in the *Commentary on the Song of Songs,* which I shall discuss next.

CHAPTER 12

A CASE STUDY OF POINTS OF CONTACT: *ORATIO* 15 OF GREGORY OF NYSSA'S *COMMENTARY ON THE SONG OF SONGS*

In the Origenist tradition, while sanctification is effected through the action of the Holy Spirit in the regenerative waters of baptism, there is a sense in which the growth into Christian discipleship which follows is primarily an effort of the person through the recovery of innate faculties, the 'wings of the soul'. While in Plato and Plotinus, these are pre-existent and immortal, for the Cappadocians they are part of the human potential which Adam and Eve squandered when they disobeyed their Creator and became absorbed in self-idolatry. In this sense the 'wings of the soul' may be understood as a metaphor for the image and likeness of God which Adam lost and can be recovered in union with Christ, the New Adam.

In Gregory's mystical writings, these inborn wings, now awakened to rationality and spiritual insight, aid the progress of the person towards virtue and moral perfection. Apart from Oratio 15, there is to my knowledge only one other reference in the Gregorian corpus where the 'wings of the soul' are clearly identified with the 'power of the Holy Spirit'.[1] This passage in *On Virginity* refers to 'the wings of a dove' from Psalm 54(55):7. Gregory asks how the soul can ascend to the heights to contemplate intelligible Beauty and answers with Scripture:

> 'There is one vehicle for the human soul for the journey to the heavens, and that is by linking itself to the cowering dove whose wings the prophet David longed for.'

In the *Macriana*, there are several references to this biblical phrase 'wings of a dove' from Psalm 54:7(55:6).[2] It could be argued either that these analogies were dependent upon Gregory' s encomium or conversely, that Gregory reworked a Macarian image for escaping 'an evil wind' into a symposium upon the ascent of the soul. That both writers were simply citing a well known Psalm and linking the imagery of the dove by association to the

1. *De Virginitate*, *PG*. 46.364A-369B, (ed., J. P. Cavarnos, *GNO* 8.1), E. trans., V. W. Callahan, *Saint Gregory of Nyssa: Ascetical Works* (Catholic Univ. of America, 1967), pp. 40-41.
2. *Macarian Homilies* II.2.3; 44.5.77; III 16.1.3; 1.2.2.

Holy Spirit seems more likely. But that Gregory was beginning to give more weight to the role of the Holy Spirit in the progress of the soul does mark a shift in his teaching which becomes marked in the following.

Gregory' s *Commentary on the Song of Songs* is a collection of homiletic interpretations of the biblical love-song cycle, which drew its allegorical method and thematic inspiration from Origen's *Commentary*, written in Athens and Caesarea in Palestine in the 240's AD.[3] Since Origen's composition after Song of Songs 2:15 has been lost, any discussion of the influence of his later textual interpretation upon Gregory's commentary must be hypothetical. What is clear is that both interpreted the Shulammite bride as the faithful soul (although Origen also linked her collectively to Mother Church[4]). In Gregory's exposition of the biblical love-song, the bride is compared to a 'little dove' by her divine lover/bridegroom, the Word or Christ. He draws her heavenwards on an ascent towards the Good and the Beautiful. which leads to a mystical interpretation of a growing identification between the bride-soul and 'the Dove' (ἡ περιστερά). For example, Gregory's commentary on 'Arise, come, my love, my beautiful one, my dove' (Song of Songs 2:13-14) is as follows:

> 'We see the Word, then, leading the bride up a rising staircase, as it were, up to the heights by the ascent of perfection. The Word first sends forth a ray of light through the windows of the Prophets and through the lattices of the Law and the commandments. Then He bids the bride draw near to the light and then to become beautiful by being changed, in the light, into the form of the Dove.'[5]

Jean Daniélou, in his lyrical commentary, interprets this and similar passages in terms of a series of transformations of the bride as she progresses in stages of 'stretching out' (ἐπέκτασις) towards perfection 'from Dove to Dove'.[6] He claims that there is a 'fundamental unity in all these texts in which Gregory develops in various ways the theme of the transformation into the Dove'[7]. Whether the Dove is the Holy Spirit or the recovery of the bride's true humanity in the image and likeness of God is a moot point.

3. Latin trans. by Rufinus of Bk. 1-3 & part of Bk.4, (*P.G.* 17.253-88), E. trans., R.P. Lawson , *Origen:*
The Song of Songs: Commentary and Homilies (Ancient Christian Writers No.26, London, Longmans, Green & Co., 1957).

4. R.P. Lawson comments, that there is a growing shift of emphasis in Origen's commentary from the union of Christ with his Church to the union between the Divine Word and the Soul, although the two remain inseparable. See, Ibid., pp. 14-15.

5. Gregory of Nyssa, *Homiliae in Canticum canticorum* (*PG* 44.873C-876C), ed. H. Langerbeck, *GNO* 6, E. trans., H. Musurillo, *From Glory to Glory: Texts from Gregory of Nyssa's Mystical Writings* (New York, SVS Press, 2001), p. 190.

6. J. Daniélou, 'Introduction', *From Glory to Glory*, p. 68.

7. Ibid., p. 69.

Meredith claims that the Holy Spirit is 'barely mentioned at all' in *On the Song*; for the action of the Dove is so identified with the moral progress of the individual that only 'a purely formal role' is left for divine grace.[8]

It certainly seems to be the case, that Gregory's interpretation focuses upon the subject's ascetic, mental and moral effort to attain likeness to Christ through imitation. In his commentary upon the biblical text, 'I to my beloved and my beloved to me' (Song of Songs 6:3), he wrote:

> 'This is the standard definition of perfection in virtue. By these words we are taught that we should have nothing other that God within us and that the purified soul should look to nothing beyond itself. It ought to be so cleansed of every filthy deed and thought, and be completely transferred into the world of intellect and immateriality and so transform itself into the most exact reflection of absolute beauty .... In the same way, she who says, "I to my beloved and my beloved to me", confesses her own beauty, the primal blessedness of her nature, has been transformed into Christ.' (Romans 8:29; Genesis 1:26).[9]

It is clearly possible to interpret these allegorical passages from different pneumatological perspectives. What is of significance for this study is the sense that in Gregory's last great spiritual commentary, there is a new emphasis upon increasing co-operation (*synergeia)* between the efforts of the faithful soul and the presence of the Spirit. This is imaged as receiving the wings of a dove and thus becoming united with the ascending Spirit Dove, 'from glory to glory'. While there are no specific parallels in the *Macarian Homilies*, there is a sense of affinity suggesting a possible sharing of imagery and spiritual vision.

In the final homily of *On the Song*,[10] there is an interpretation which comes closest to the Macarian cluster of spiritual themes connected to the 'wings of the Spirit'. After discussing Scriptural references to the wings of God, 'our prototype', Gregory described Adam's fall from Paradise as a loss of wings, in language reminiscent of Origen[11] and the myth in Plato's, *Phaedrus*.[12] He then referred to his own salvation:

> 'By Thine eyes, O Lord, I obtain the grace of being winged again, of recovering through virtue the wings of the Dove, by which I may have the power of flight.'

8. A. Meredith, 'The Pneumatology of the Cappadocian Fathers', p. 208.

9. *Oratio* 6,3, *Hom. in* Canticum , Eng. trans., Gregory Meredith, *Gregory of Nyssa*, p. 113.

10. *Oratio* 15, *Hom. in Canticum* (*PG* 44.1100C-1120A), ed. H. Langerbeck, *GNO* 6, pp. 447-470, E. trans., H. Musurillo, pp. 284-288.

11. For Origen, (and for Gregory in this passage), man lost his 'likeness' to God by losing his wings. See, *De Principiis* 3.4.1.

12. Plato, *Phaedrus* 246; See also, Plotinus, *Ennead* 4.8.1.

There follows a commentary on verses from Song of Songs 6:8: 'One is my dove, my perfect one: she is the only one of her mother, the chosen one of her who bore her.' Here, there is a discussion of the unity of Christians that Christ prayed for in his last discourse (John 17:21-22). This unity, Gregory interpreted as 'participation in the glory of the Spirit', by which the Incarnation was restored to human nature and is communicated to all who are united with Christ the Bridegroom. He then enquired: who is the 'perfect dove' which the Bridegroom seeks in the Canticle and who is her mother? At this point he clearly identified the Holy Spirit as the mother Dove of the dove of the beloved bride:

> 'If the offspring is a dove, then surely its mother must be that Dove that came down from heaven to the Jordan as John testifies. This is the Dove that the maidens call blessed, and the queens and concubines praise (Song of Songs 6:8). For the path to that blessed happiness is one that is open to all souls from every rank .... So the daughters bless the Dove. And they too would desire above all to become doves.'[13]

There are several similarities between this sermon and the Macarian themes connected with the 'wings of the Spirit'. While 'the dove' is a feminine noun in Greek, the play on the gender to link her presence with the Holy Spirit as a mother of the bride-soul is a surprising innovation for Gregory who, in his *On Virginity* tended to denigrate mothering functions. In particular, his emphasis upon an image of a mother-bird and her offspring, and a progressive ascent on the wings of the Dove suggest points of contact with the parable of the 'Mother Bird and Her Fledglings' in *Collection* III.16. Vincent Desprez argues that this entire Macarian homily shows dependency upon Gregory's *Commentary on the Song.* In my opinion, while it is possible that there was some mutual influence, it cannot be claimed that Gregory's abstract symbol of the mother Dove could be the source of the mothering description in the Macarian homily:

> 'First of all, at the beginning, hearts are fed with spiritual milk which is full of gentleness and heavenly affection, ... Peter says, "As infants newly born, you desire spiritual milk."(1 Peter 2:2). Afterwards, gradually in proportion to progress in the growth and renewal of the soul, the Spirit gives more solid food, and at the same time the wings of grace. That is to say, the power of the Spirit grows in the soul as it progresses in good works. Next, Divine Grace, the good and heavenly Mother, teaches the mind to fly. First of all, around the nest of the heart or the thoughts. That is to say, to pray to God without distractions through spiritual power.'[14]

13. *Hom.in Canticorum*, *Oratio* 15, E. trans., Musurillo, pp. 287-8.
14. Collection III.16.2.3-2.5.

This Macarian emphasis upon the brooding, protecting, feeding, gentle nurturing, teaching and guidance of the mother-bird in the Macarian analogy stresses the agency of loving divine grace and the vulnerability of the infant children of God. The Gregorian eulogy to the mother Dove inspires the Christian daughters to contemplate her beauty and desire her imitation. The Macarian emphasis is upon loving divine initiative, and the dependence of the believer on sacramental grace to mature. The Gregorian teaching focuses upon personal transformation through a progressive yearning for the prototype Dove.

The claim Desprez made above for Macarian dependency is also partly based upon Macarian familiarity with 'patristic', bride and bridegroom imagery and 'the spirit of the *Song*'.[15] But such a claim overlooks the alternative Syriac traditions I have explored in this study. In Ephrem' s hymnody for example, baptism is often described as the betrothal of the consecrated 'virgin' bride with Christ the bridegroom (*Hatnâ*) and as entry into the bridal chamber of the heart (*gnônâ*).[16] In the Syriac ritual, the female baptismal candidate was crowned before entering the water to symbolise the marriage of her soul to Christ.[17]

I would highlight one fundamental difference between Gregory's emphasis upon the Holy Spirit as the Dove and Macarian usage. For although Macarius does sometimes use dove imagery, it is always in the context of a reference to a Psalm or Jewish sacrificial practices or as a simile for innocence and purity (the dove was popularly believed to have no bile duct!). In the analogies of the Holy Spirit as a mother-bird, a dove is never mentioned, although in one analogy he does use the example of a 'swallow' (ἡ χελιδών).[18] The reason, as discussed earlier, is the Syriac emphasis upon the dynamic and creative nature of the mother Spirit's *wings* over the waters, which is in marked contrast to the reified symbol of the Spirit-Dove in Hellenistic Christianity. Thus in the Macarian account of the 'appearance of the Spirit of God on Jesus' at his baptism in the River Jordan, the image of the Spirit 'in the form of a dove' is not mentioned.[19]

The question of the precise relationship between *Oratio* 15 and Macarian teaching on the 'wings of the Spirit' cannot be answered conclusively. This

15. V. Desprez, *Pseudo-Macaire*, p. 61, n.2.
16. See, S. Brock, 'The Bridal Chamber of the Heart', in, *The Luminous Eye*, pp. 115-130.
17. Robert Murray, *Symbols of Church and Kingdom*, p. 141.
18. *Macarian Homilies*, III.27.4.1, ed., V. Desprez, pp. 322-3.
19. *Macarian Homilies* I. 3.5.9-3.6.1, ed. H. Berthold, *Symeon-Makarios: Reden und Briefe*, pp. 39-40.

study has demonstrated that it is plausible to derive the Macarian metaphor for the presence and power of the Holy Spirit, consistently from a Syriac Christian tradition. If the scholarly consensus since Jaeger is correct however, and Macarian 'wings language' is dependent upon a Gregorian interpretation of the Platonic 'wings of the soul' one would expect the cluster of themes connected with the Macarian 'wings of the Spirit' to be clearly evident in Gregory's writings. I have demonstrated that, to the contrary, only *Oratio* 15 shares some of these features. In my opinion, while there are some similarities, there are also differences and many omissions of basic Macarian wings teaching. Logically, this cannot be the only or indeed primary source for the over twenty-five references to the 'wings of the Spirit' in the *Macarian Homilies*.

In conclusion, there do seem to be some points of contact, suggesting a convergence of interests and a mutuality of influence between Gregory and Macarius. Given that Gregory had read the *Great Letter* and, indeed, rewritten it for a cultured Greek audience, we can speculate that he may have also read other homilies connected with the same spiritual elder. Conversely, Macarius may have read the *Commentary on the Song* and incorporated some of its noetic and flight imagery into his later teachings. The very fluidity of the Syriac metaphor of the 'wings of the Spirit' as interpreted and translated by the wordsmith Macarius made it a flexible spiritual symbol which could function as a bridge between Greek and Syriac cultural and religious traditions.

Ὦ πτέρυγες ἡπλωμέναι, ὦ σπλάγχνα πατρός. Ἀμήν.[20]

20. *Macarian Homilies*, I. 3.6.4, ed. H. Berthold, *Symeon-Makarios: Reden und Briefe*, p. 41.

ABBREVIATIONS

CSCO	*Corpus Scriptorum Christianorum Orientalium* (gen. ed. Beck, Edmund, Louvain, 1950-)
GCS	Die griechischen christlichen Schriftsteller der ersten drei Jahrhunderte (Berlin).
GNO	Gregory of Nyssa, *Gregorii Nysseni Opera* (Leiden, Brill, 1960-).
PG	Migne, Jacques-Paul, *Patrologia Graeca* (Paris, 1857-1866).
PS 1	Graffin, R., *Patrologia Syriaca* (Paris, 1894).
PS 3	Kmosko, M., *Patrologica Syrica* (Paris, 1926).
SS	*Scriptores Syri* (subdivision of CSCO).

BIBLIOGRAPHY

A. Primary Sources and Translations

ACTS OF THOMAS

James, Montague (tr. Greek text, Bonnet, 1903), in: *The Apocryphal New Testament* (Oxford, Clarendon Press, 1st edition,1924, reprint with revisions, 1975), 364-438.

APHRAHAT THE PERSIAN SAGE

Brock, Sebastian (tr. PS 1 cols.137-82), *Demonstration 4: On Prayer*, in: *The Syriac Fathers on Prayer and the Spiritual Life* (Kalamazoo, Cistercian Publications, 1987), 5-28.

Gwynn, John (tr.), *Demonstrations 1, 5, 6, 8, 10, 17, 21-22,* in: *Gregory the Great, Ephraim Syrus and Aphrahat the Persian Sage* (Nicene and Post-Nicene Fathers; 2nd Series, 13, 1898, reprint, Grand Rapids, Eerdmans, 1976), 345-412.

Neusner, Jacob (tr.), *Demonstrations 1,5, 11-13, 15-21, 23*, in: *Aphrahat and Judaism: The Christian-Jewish Argument in Fourth-Century Iran* (Studia Post-Biblica; Leiden, Brill, 1971), 13-133.

Parisot, D.I. (ed.), *Aphraatis Sapientis Persae Demonstrationes 1-23* (tr. 1 & 2, Paris 1894, 1907), cols. 1–489.

BASIL OF CAESAREA

Anderson, John (tr. PG 32 68-217), *On the Holy Spirit* (Crestwood, New York, SVS Press, 1980).

Giet, S., (ed.), *Homiliae in Hexaemeron* 2.6., (SC 26, Paris 1968), 166-71.

BOOK OF STEPS (LIBER GRADUUM)

Brock, Sebastian (tr. PS 3 cols. 285-304), *Discourse 12: On the Ministry of the Hidden and the Manifest Church*; (tr. PS 3 cols. 433-44), *Discourse 18: On the Tears of Prayer,* in: *The Syriac Fathers on Prayers and the Spiritual Life* (Kalamazoo, Cistercian Publications, 1987), 45-53 & 54-9.

Kitchen, Robert A. & Parmentier, M.F.G (tr.), *The Book of Steps* (Kalamazoo, Cistercian Publications, 2005).

EPHREM THE SYRIAN

Brock, Sebastian, (tr. CSCO 174-5 = SS 78-9), *Hymns on Paradise;* (tr. CSCO 152 = SS 71); *Commentary on Genesis 2-3* (New York, Crestwood, SVS Press, 1998).

Brock, Sebastian, *The Harp of the Spirit: Eighteen Poems of Saint Ephrem* (Studies Supplementary to *Sobornost* 4; 2nd edition, London, 1983).

McVey, Kathleen, (tr. CSCO 174-5 = SS 78-9), *Hymns against Julian;*(tr. CSCO 186-7 = SS 82-3), *Hymns on the Nativity;* (tr. CSCO 223-4 = SS 94-5), *Hymns on Virginity*, in: *Ephrem the Syrian: Hymns* (Classics of Western Spirituality; Mahwah, Paulist Press,1989).

Gwynn, John (tr. PG 46 cols.819-49), *De vita Ephraemi Syri, Selections translated into English from the Hymns and Homilies of Ephraim the Syrian* (Select Library of Nicene and Post-Nicene Fathers of the Christian Church, series 2, 13; part II, Oxford/New York, 1898, reprint, Grand Rapids, Eerdmans, 1976), 124-38.

Gwynn, John (tr. Roman text), *Nisibene Hymns 1-21, 35-42 and 52-68; Hymns on Epiphany 1-15,* in: *Selections translated into English from the Hymns and Homilies of Ephraim the Syrian* (Select Library of Nicene and Post-Nicene Fathers of the Christian Church; series 2, 13; part II, Oxford/New York, 1898, reprint, Grand Rapids, Eerdmans, 1976).

Mathews, Edward, (tr. CSCO 152 + SS 7) *Commentary on Genesis* (tr. Brit. Lib. Add. 7190, ff. 188-193); *Letter to Publius*, in: Kathleen McVey (ed.), *St Ephrem the Syrian: Selected Prose Works* (Fathers of the Church 91; Washington, Catholic University of America Press, 1994), 67-213 & 338-55.

Morris, J.B (tr. Roman text), *Hymns on Faith 81-7 (The Pearl)*, in: *Select Works of St. Ephrem the Syrian* (Oxford, 1847).

Murray, Robert (tr. CSCO 154 =SS 73), *Hymn on Faith 10*, in: 'A Hymn of St Ephrem to Christ on the Incarnation, the Holy Spirit, and the Sacraments', *Eastern Churches Review* 3 (1970):142-50.

Murray, Robert (tr. CSCO 154 = SS 73), *Hymn of Faith 74 (On the Holy Spirit)*, in: *Symbols of Church and Kingdom: A Study in Early Syriac Tradition* (London, T. &. T. Clark, revised edition, 2006), 80-1.

GREGORY OF NYSSA

Callahan, Virginia. W. (tr. GNO 8), *On Perfection, On the Christian Profession, On the Soul and Resurrection, On Virginity, On What it Means to call Oneself a Christian, The Life of Macrina,* in: *Saint Gregory of Nyssa: Ascetical Works* (Fathers of the Church 58; Washington, Howard University, 1967).

Daniélou, Jean (intro.) & Musurillo, Herbert, (tr.), *From Glory to Glory: Texts from Gregory of Nyssa's Mystical Writings* (New York, 1961, reprint, Crestwood, New York, SVS Press, 2001).

Graef, Hilda., (tr. GNO 7.239ff), *The Lords Prayer*; (tr. PG. 44.1193-1302) *The Beatitudes* (Ancient Christian Writers18; London, Catholic University of America,1954).

Heine, Ronald (tr. GNO 5), *Treatise on the Inscriptions of the Psalms* (Oxford Early Christian Studies; Oxford, Clarendon Press, 1995).

Langerbeck, Hermannus, (ed. GNO 6), *Homiliae in Canticum canticorum.*

Malherbe, Abraham J., & Ferguson, Everett (tr. GNO 7.1), *The Life of Moses* (Classics of Western Spirituality; Mahwah, Paulist Press, 1978).

Meredith, Anthony (tr.), (GNO 3.1.105.19-110.23), *Against the Macedonians, On the Holy Spirit 19-26*; (GNO 6.440ff.), *Commentary on the Song of Songs 15 on Song 6.1-9,* in: *Gregory of Nyssa* (Early Church Fathers; London, Routledge, 1999), 39-46 & 109-28.

Staats, Reinhold (ed. GNO 8), *De Instituto Christiano*, in: *Makarios-Symeon: Epistola Magna. Eine messalianische Mönchsregel und ihre Umschrift in Gregors von Nyssa 'De Instituto Christiano'* (Göttingen, 1984).

MACARIUS-SYMEON

Berthold, Heinz, (ed. I. *logoi* 2-64), *Makarios/Symeon: Reden und Briefe: Die Sammlung I des Vaticanus Graecus 694 (B)*, 2 vols. (GCS 55-6; Berlin, Akademie Verlag, 1973).

Desprez, Vincent, (ed. & tr. III), *Pseudo-Macaire: Oeuvres spirituelles, I: Homélies propres à la Collection III* (Sources Chrétiennes 275; Paris, 1980).

Maloney, George, (tr. II), *Pseudo-Macarius: The Fifty Spiritual Homilies and the Great Letter* (Classics of Western Spirituality; Mahwah, Paulist Press, 1992).

St Nikodimos of the Holy Mountain and St Makarios of Corinth (ed. IV: PG 34 841-965), 'St Symeon Metaphrastis' Paraphrase of the Homilies of St Makarios of Egypt' ('The 150 Chapters'), in: *The Philokalia Vol. III trans.* G.E.H. Palmer, Philip Sherrard & Kallistos Ware (London, Faber & Faber, 1984), 285-353.

Staats, Reinhold, (ed. I. *logos* 1, *Epistola Magna*). In, *Makarios-Symeon: Epistola Magna. Eine messalianische Mönchsregel und ihre Umschrift in Gregors von Nyssa 'De Instituto Christiano'* (Göttingen, 1984).

ODES OF SOLOMON

Charlesworth, James H. (ed. & tr.), *The Odes of Solomon* (Chico, Scholars Press, 1982).

ORIGEN

Greer, Rowan, (tr.), *An Exhortation to Martyrdom, First Principles: Book IV, Prologue to the Commentary on the Song of Songs*, in: *Origen: An Exhortation to Martyrdom, Prayer and Selected Works* (Classics of Western Spirituality; Mahwah, Paulist Press, 1979).

Lawson, R.P. (tr. Latin text, ed. W. Baehrens, GCS Vol.8, 1957), *The Song of Songs: Commentary and Homilies* (Ancient Christian Writers 26; London, Longmans, Green & Co.,1957).

TEACHING OF ADDAI

Howard, George (tr.), *The Teaching of Addai* (SBL Texts and Translations 16: Early Christian Literature Series 4; Michigan, Scholars Press, 1981).

B. General and Secondary Sources

Baker, Aelred, 'Pseudo-Macarius and the Gospel of Thomas', *Vigiliae Christianae* 1(1964): 215-25.

Id., 'Pseudo-Macarius and Gregory of Nyssa', *Vigiliae Christianae* 20 (1966): 227-34.

Beck, Edmund, 'Die Eucharistie bei Ephräm', *Oriens Christianus* 38 (1954): 41-67.
Id., 'Symbolum-Mysterium bei Aphraat und Ephräm', *Oriens Christianus* 42 (1958): 19-40.
Beggiani, Seely, *Early Syriac Theology: With Special Reference to the Maronite Tradition* (London, Univ. Press of America, 1983).
Id., *Introduction to Eastern Christian Spirituality: The Syriac Tradition* (London, Assoc. Univ. Presses, 1991).
Brock, Sebastian, 'Mary and the Eucharist: an Oriental Perspective', *Sobernost/ Eastern Churches Review* 1: 2 (1979): 50-59.
Id., 'The Syrian Baptismal Rite', *Concilium* vol.22 (1979): 98-104.
Id., 'The Holy Spirit as Feminine in Early Syriac Literature', in Janet M. Soskice (ed.), *After Eve: Women, Theology and the Christian Tradition* (London, Marshall Pickering, 1990), 73-87.
Id., *The Luminous Eye: The Spiritual World Vision of Saint Ephrem the Syrian* (Cistercian Study Series124; Kalamazoo, Michigan, 1992).
Id., 'Eusebius and Syriac Christianity', in H.W. Attridge and G. Hata (eds.), *Eusebius, Christianity and Judaism* (Detroit, Yamamoto Shoten 1992), 212-34.
Id., *Studies in Syriac Christianity: History, Literature and Theology* (Variorum Collected Studies Series: Aldershot, Ashgate Pub., 1992).
Id., 'Greek and Syriac in Late Antique Syria', in A.K Bowman & G. Woolf (eds.), *Literacy and Power in the Ancient World* (Cambridge, Cambridge University Press,1994), 149-60.
Id., *From Ephrem to Romanos: Interactions between Syriac and Greek in Late Antiquity* (Variorum Collected Studies Series; Aldershot, Ashgate, 1999).

Coakley, Sarah, *Powers and Submissions: Spirituality, Philosophy and Gender* (Challenges in Contemporary Theology; Malden, Mass., Blackwell Publishing, 2002).

Daniélou, Jean, 'Introduction' to *From Glory to Glory: Texts from Gregory of Nyssa's Mystical Writings* (reprint, New York, SVS Press, 2001), 3-78.
Desprez, Vincent, 'Introduction' to *Pseudo-Macaire: Oeuvres spirituelle, I: Homélies propres à la Collection III* (Sources Chrétiennes 275; Paris, 1992), 1-63.
Dörries, Hermann, *Symeon von Mesopotamien. Die Überlieferung der messalianischen Makarios-Scriften* (Texte und Untersuchungen 55/ 1; Leipzig-Berlin, 1941).
Drijvers, Hendrijk J.W., *East of Antioch: Studies in Early Syriac Christianity* (London, Variorum, 1984).

Fedwick, Paul J., *The Church and the Charisma of Leadership in Basil of Caesarea* (Toronto, Pontifical Institute of Mediaeval Studies, 1979).

Gero, Stephen, 'The Spirit as a Dove at the Baptism of Jesus', *Novum Testamentum* 18/1 (1976): 17-35.
Golitzin, Alexander, 'Temple and Throne of the Divine Glory: "Pseudo-Macarius" and Purity of Heart, Together with some Remarks on the Limitations and Usefulness of Scholarship,' in: H.A. Luckman & L.Kulzer (eds.), *Purity of Heart in Early Ascetic and Monastic Literature* (Minnesota, The Liturgical Press, 1999), 107-30.

Id., 'Recovering the "Glory of Adam": "Divine Light" Traditions in the Dead Sea Scrolls and the Christian Ascetical Literature of Fourth-Century Syro-Mesopotamia', in James R. Davila (ed.), *The Dead Sea Scrolls as Background to Post-biblical Judaism and Early Christianity* (Studies on the Texts of the Desert of Judah 46; Leiden, Brill, 2003), 275-308.

Gribomont, Jean, 'Le De instituto christiano et le Messalianisme de Grégoire de Nysse', *Studia Patristica* 5 (Berlin, 1962): 312-22.

Haar Romeny, R.B., ter, *A Syrian in Greek Dress; The Use of Greek, Hebrew and Syriac Biblical Texts in Eusebius of Emesa' s Commentary on Genesis* (Traditio Exegetica Graeca 6; Leuven, Peeters,1997).

Harvey, Susan A., 'Feminine Imagery of the Divine: The Holy Spirit, the Odes of Solomon and Early Syriac Tradition', *St. Vladimir's Theological Quarterly* Vol.37/2; 8 (1993):111-39.

Himmelfarb, Martha, *Ascent to Heaven in Jewish and Christian Apocalypses* (New York, Oxford University Press, 1993).

Jaeger, Werner, *Two Rediscovered Works Of Ancient Christian Literature: Gregory of Nyssa and Macarius* (Leiden, Brill, 1954).

Id., *Early Christianity and Greek Paideia* (London, OUP, 1962).

Jansma, Taeke, 'Investigations into the Early Syrian Fathers On Genesis', in *Studies on the Book of Genesis, Oudtestamentische Studien* 12 (1958): 69-181.

Keck, Leander E., 'The Spirit and the Dove', *New Testament Studies* 17 (1970-71): 41-67.

Kitchen, Robert A. & Parmentier, Martien F.G., 'Introduction', to *The Book of Steps: The Syriac Liber Graduum* (Kalamazoo, Cistercian Pub., 2005): xiii-lxxxiii.

Klijn, Albertus F.J., 'Some Remarks on the Quotations of the Gospels in Gregory of Nyssa's, "De Instituto Christiano" and Macarius' "Epistola Magna"', *Vigiliae Christianae* 19 (1965): 164-68.

Louth, Andrew, *The Origins of the Christian Mystical Tradition: From Plato to Denys* (revised edition, Oxford, OUP, 2007).

Maloney, George, 'Introduction' to, *Pseudo-Macarius: The Fifty Spiritual Homilies and the Great Letter* (Classics of Western Spirituality; Mahwah, Paulist Press, 1992), 1-35.

McGuckin, John A., *Standing in God's Holy Fire: The Byzantine Tradition* (Traditions of Christian Spirituality Series; London, Darton, Longman and Todd, 2001).

McNeil, B., 'The Odes of Solomon and the Scriptures', *Oriens Christianus* 67 (1983): 104-22.

Meredith, Anthony, 'The Pneumatology of the Cappadocian Fathers and the Creed of Constantinople', *Irish Theological Quarterly* 48 (1981):196-211.

Id., *Gregory of Nyssa* (Early Church Fathers; London, Routledge, 1999).

Id., *The Cappadocians* (London, 1995).

Murray, Robert, 'A Hymn of St Ephrem to Christ on the Incarnation, the Holy Spirit and the Sacraments', *Eastern Churches Review* 3 (1970): 142-50.

Id., 'The Exhortation to Candidates for Ascetical Vows at Baptism in the Ancient Syrian Church', *New Testament Studies* 21 (1974-5): 59-80.
Id., 'Some Themes and Problems of Early Syriac Angeology', *Symposium Syriacum*, 1988 (ed. R. Lavenant; OCA 236; Rome, Pontifical Institute of Oriental Studies, 1990), 143-53.
Id., *Symbols of Church and Kingdom: A Study in Early Syriac Tradition* (revised edition, London, T.& T. Clark, 2006).

Narinskaya, Elena, *Ephrem, a 'Jewish Sage'? A Comparison of the Exegetical Writings of St. Ephrem the Syrian and Jewish Traditions* (Studia Traditionis Theologiae 7, Turnhout, Brepols, 2010).
Nedungatt, George, 'The Covenanters of the Early Syriac-Speaking Church', *Orientalia Christiana Periodica* 39 (1973), 191-215 & 419-44.
Neusner, Jacob, *Aphrahat and Judaism: The Christian-Jewish Argument in Fourth-Century Iran* (Studia Post-Biblica; Leiden, Brill, 1971).

Plested, Marcus, *The Macarian Legacy: The Place of Macarius-Symeon in the Eastern Christian Tradition* (Oxford Theological Monographs; Oxford, OUP, 2004).

Quispel, Gilles, 'The Syrian Thomas and the Syrian Macarius', *Vigiliae Christianae* 18 (1964): 226-35.

Rousseau, O., 'Le rencontre de S. Ephrem et de S. Basile', *L'Orient Syrien* 2 (1957): 261-84.
Russell, Norman, *The Doctrine of Deification in the Greek Patristic Tradition* (Oxford Early Christian Studies; Oxford, OUP, 2004).

Scholem, Gershom, *Major Trends in Jewish Mysticism*, 3rd revised edition (Jerusalem, Scocken Publishing House, 1973).
Schüngel-Straumann, Helen, *Rûach bewegt die Welt* (Stuttgarter Bibelstudien 151; Stuttgart, Katholisches Bibelwerk GmbH, 1992).
Schroer, Silvia, 'Der Geist, die Weisheit und die Taube', *Freiburger Zeitschrift für Philosophie und Theologie* 33 (1986): 197-225.
Staats, Reinhold, 'Die Asketen aus Mesopotamien in der Rede des Gregor von Nyssa in *suam ordinationem*', *Vigiliae Christianae* 21 (1967): 165-79.
Stewart, Columba, *'Working the Earth of the Heart': The Messalian Controversy in History, Texts and Language to AD 431* (Oxford Theological Monographs; Oxford, Clarendon Press, 1991).

Van Rompay, Luk, 'L'informateur Syrien de Basile de Césarée. A propos de Genèse 1,2', *Orientalia Christiana Periodica* 58 (1992): 245-51.
Vööbus, Arthur, *Literary-Critical and Historical Studies in Ephrem the Syrian* (The Estonian Theological Society in Exile 10; Sweden, Stockholm, 1958).

Ware, Kallistos, 'Preface' to G. Maloney, trans., *Pseudo-Macarius: The Fifty Spiritual Homilies and the Great Letter* (Classics of Western Spirituality; Mahwah, Paulist Press, 1992), xi-xviii.
Weitzman, Michael, *The Syriac Version of the Old Testament: An Introduction* (Cambridge, 1999).